Worship
in the Shape of
Scripture

Worship
in the Shape of
Scripture

Revised and Updated

F. Russell Mitman

THE
PILGRIM
PRESS
Cleveland

For John R. Weiler and William R. Swisher Jr.
Mentors and Colleagues in Ministry

The Pilgrim Press, Cleveland, Ohio 44115
www.pilgrimpress.com

Printed in the United States of America on acid-free paper

14   13   12   11   5   4   3   2

Library of Congress Cataloging-in-Publication Data

Mitman, F. Russell
    Worship in the shape of Scripture / F. Russell Mitman.
       p.   cm.
    Includes bibliographical references.
    ISBN 0-8298-1421-3 (pbk. : alk. paper)
    ISBN 978-0-8298-1826-0 (alk. paper; revised edition)
    1. Public worship – United Church of Christ. 2. Worship programs – Planning.
  3. Liturgics. 4. United Church of Christ – Liturgy. 5. United Church of Christ –
  Doctrines. I. Title.
  BX9886.M58 2001
    264′.05834 – dc21   00-054856

Contents

Foreword

I experienced this book before I read it. It was my privilege to encounter God through worship under Russell Mitman's leadership at a clergy gathering of the Pennsylvania Southeast Conference he serves. That event and the intrigue stirred by his title, *Worship in the Shape of Scripture,* made me look forward eagerly to reading this volume. I was not disappointed.

Mitman's extensive background prepared him to write what churches and their leaders need. He has served as a pastor for twenty-seven years and now cares for many other pastors and congregations as a regional Conference Minister in the United Church of Christ. His deep spirituality was very evident in the few days I was with him and in the comments of his co-workers; similarly, it shines in this volume.

But you might wonder, why do we need another book about worship? There seems to be a plethora of publications on that subject these days.

Mitman's book is unique for several reasons, perhaps most important of which is that his is rooted deeply in the Hebrew and Christian Scriptures, as the "normative and definitive text" for shaping worship. Having done his historical homework carefully, Mitman demonstrates how the structure common to the worship of most denominations is rooted in the Scriptures themselves. His delineation and exposition of this structure are more than sufficient reasons to read this volume.

However, this is just the beginning. Mitman not only bemoans the lack of biblical training in churches; he actually does something about it.

He certainly doesn't do pastors' and churches' work for them, but he equips us all with motivation, understandings, and examples to enable us to craft appropriate worship expressions for our particular place and people. In the process he links the ancient heritage of the so-called "liturgical" churches with the gifts of the "free church" traditions.

Though Mitman has engaged in ministry primarily in the "free church" realm and writes especially for those who participate in it, he has much to teach those of us whose worship practices derive more directly from catholic sources. His bridging ideas enable us all to appreciate and appropriate the best gifts of the church's worship throughout time and space. Particularly, his focus, stated with his typically memorable phrasing, is to provide his colleagues with "some markers and suggestions" that delineate the process whereby worship leaders "need not feel they are lobbing liturgical tennis balls at a blank wall."

Mitman's writing delights us with many such quotable phrases — "leaders give away attention"; "Not improvisation but abdication" — which I've already found myself repeating in lectures. He also cites many of the best thinkers engaged in worship issues. It is very obvious that Mitman has read extensively and has contemplated the literature thoroughly.

His comprehensive study and years of practical crafting combine to generate clarifying explanations and helpful examples of the *organic* liturgy Mitman advocates. Frequently I found myself truly worshiping simply by reading his models. Some of us might work more easily with theoretical foundations; others of us are more concerned with the practical. In this book you won't want to skip either.

In the process of describing the transposing of Scripture and the shaping, orchestrating, and doing of worship, Mitman widens our understanding of numerous elements such as proclamation, liturgy, confessions, the Word, rhetoric, translucence, worship leadership, the bearing of leaders, change, and language. He achieves great poise in many tricky dialectical tensions such as the worship fulcrum of "local assembly" and "universal communion" (to use Gordon Lathrop's terms), the pressures of new versus old, or the encountering of human with divine.

Readers might not agree with every single thing Mitman writes as he discusses attire, space, bearing and gestures, the size of the Bible, silence, bulletins, announcements, and other aspects or accoutrements of worship, but he raises essential questions in this book about broad themes and even housekeeping chores that each worshiping community should consider for the sake of faithful praise. The range of worship dimensions deftly handled is quite exceptional.

Yet through them all Mitman never forgets the lesson of a painting by Louis Cranach the Elder which he describes and which I will only mention here to tantalize you. It is a lesson that many churches seem to be forgetting these days and need desperately to recover to keep their liturgy (of whatever form) open to its inherent purpose and to prevent any hindrances to genuine praise.

Mitman offers his best to help us remember. We owe him enormous gratitude!

MARVA J. DAWN
author of *A Royal "Waste" of Time* and
Reaching Out without Dumbing Down

Preface

What appears on the following pages is the result of more than a third of a century of ministry in a variety of settings in which I was called upon to create homiletical and liturgical expressions for worshiping congregations. Just as sermons and worship materials are shaped by the life-texts that people bring to the worship event, so also these thoughts have been forged by my ministry with congregations, teachers of the Church, lay worship leaders, and the hundreds of eager pastors and students who have been part of the workshops on worship leadership that I have led. As I preface this work I know that I am surrounded by a cloud of faithful witnesses who have shaped my ministry and have helped me discover the centrality I place on the worship life of the Church.

I wish to thank Professor W. Dow Edgerton of Chicago Theological Seminary who first urged me to pursue the theme of this book, to George R. Graham, Editorial Director for Professional and Academic Books of The Pilgrim Press, for his kind editorial assistance, and to Arthur G. Clyde for his critique of the music I composed. I am indebted to the Conference Consistory of Pennsylvania Southeast Conference of the United Church of Christ who afforded me sabbatical time to complete the manuscript, to the Conference staff who have shouldered some of my responsibilities while I devoted myself to this task, and to the hundreds of pastors and lay persons who participated in the worship services for which the worship expressions included here originally were shaped. Finally, I thank my family who have encouraged me in my homiletical and liturgical work and who have endured patiently the repetitions of sounds, some emanating from my lips as I articulated the words aloud while staring at the computer screen and others from the electronic key-board on which the music was composed. I also ask their forgiveness for the absences that workshops and all-day vigils in my study have caused. There is a rich communion of saints who have contributed in ways they do not even know to this project, and my only word to them all is, "Thanks!"

Preface to the Revised and Updated Edition

In 2001 The Pilgrim Press published the initial edition of *Worship in the Shape of Scripture*. This treatise on how to craft liturgies shaped by Scripture texts has been used by pastors and by teachers of worship in seminaries throughout the United States across the ecumenical spectrum. It also has provided ways for worship committees in local churches to be engaged in conversations about their own worship practices and has offered suggestions for liturgical renewal in a variety of settings. It has prompted many learning moments in the life of the church — seminars with clergy and worship committees, invitations for consultations in congregations, and opportunities for personal coaching with worship leaders. Each engagement has enriched me in many ways, and I have attempted to incorporate many of the insights I have gained in the text of this revised edition.

The most significant additions are the video sessions in the DVD that is included with this edition. The first session, "Worship in the Shape of Scripture," is designed for students and local church study groups to serve as an introduction to creating liturgy. It was recorded live amid a group of pastors and lay leaders interested in worship renewal, and hopefully it will spark similar conversations in other settings regarding the shaping of worship in those communities.

This first session also may serve as a pattern for leaders in local settings to adapt for their own use in teaching about worship. The outline of the "Basic Structure of a Service of Word and Sacrament Paralleled with Isaiah's Temple Vision" on page 57 may be reproduced as a hand-out or for video projection, provided the following acknowledgment is attached: "From F. Russell Mitman, *Worship in the Shape of Scripture,* Copyright © 2009 by F. Russell Mitman. Published by The Pilgrim Press. Used by permission."

The second session, "The Bulletins of Common Prayer," is designed as a practical guide to those involved in the preparation of worship resources — pastors, worship leadership teams, and church administrators. It also can be helpful to groups responsible for worship renewal in local churches. It aims to capture in video format some of the issues I address in the section headed "The Bulletins of Common Prayer" at the end of chapter 6.

I wish to thank those who participated in the video recording, and particularly Pastor Joseph Irwin, Minister of Communication for Pennsylvania Southeast Conference of the United Church of Christ, who was the videographer and editor of the DVD. To those professors and pastors, lay leaders and students, who have found the first edition valuable and have provided the insights that have helped shaped this edition I owe my sincere thanks. And, finally, to the editors of The Pilgrim Press who had the vision to publish the first edition and have committed to this revision and accompanying video presentation, I express my deep appreciation.

F. Russell Mitman

Epiphany, 2009

Worship
in the Shape of
Scripture

ONE

Releasing the Word in Worship

"Creating Sermons in the Shape of Scripture" is the subtitle of a collection of articles and sermons by several homileticians edited nearly a quarter century ago by Don Wardlaw under the title *Preaching Biblically*. In the introduction to the collection, Wardlaw wrote,

> The form of the contemporary sermon necessarily works from union with its content, namely, the Word of God in Scripture.... The sermon shape should derive itself from the content it seeks to embody and express. The passage of Scripture undergirding the sermon carries implicit signals for ways the sermon could form itself. Sermon form, then, becomes a hermeneutic in itself, releasing the scriptural Word among the hearers through the liberated expression of the preacher.[1]

Wardlaw was writing for preachers about preaching. Yet, I ask, is there also a *liturgical hermeneutic* that will release the scriptural Word among the community through the structure and expressions of the total worship event? Is it also possible to create entire worship services in the shape of Scripture? Are there inherent signals in the scriptural passages that suggest ways in which liturgical expressions and actions could form themselves?

In the working lexicons of most pastors, parishioners, and seminary professors, preaching is conceived of as a praxis of ministry devoted to the delivery of sermons. "Preaching" to those engaged actively in the art means first of all — depending on denominational, ethnic, or local traditions — putting together something to say in about twenty minutes on Sunday mornings. Or, to those more passively engaged in the preaching moment, it means putting up with something of about twenty minutes in length that is identified in some church bulletins as "sermon" or "homily" or "message" or by any other synonym designed to imply that this should be a not-too-long, but long-enough, and certainly a pleasantly endurable experience. Further, "preacher" is the one designated to do this twenty-minute thing, although in some traditions "preacher" also involves a longer job description. And in the places where preachers are prepared for preaching, most often homiletics is taught as the art of sermonizing.

Until the escapades of some TV evangelists in the latter days of the twentieth century tainted public perceptions, America has had a love affair with preachers. America's moral conscience has been shaped by preaching. Today in certain ethnic and racial communities, even amid a pervasive secularization of the culture, preachers command a shaping presence. The central role of the pulpit — if one reads American history from an East Coast perspective — is preserved in the architecture of the eighteenth- and nineteenth-century Protestant meetinghouses and churches that were duplicated from eastern ports to the western prairies. Although there were some practicalities arising from the lack of central heating and electronic sound amplification that forced architectural consequences, in most churches the pulpit was central because it was for preaching that people came to church on Sundays. Sometimes sermons were long on Sundays, and deacons with feathers on the ends of poles were deputized to awaken the dozing faithful.

Then, by the middle of the nineteenth century, something new began to capture the American Protestant mind and heart — something my mentor, the late James Hastings Nichols, who taught church history at Princeton Theological Seminary, labeled "Romanticism."[2] Romanticism has received many definitions, but perhaps one that fits best in discussions on worship and preaching has to do with romanticism as an appreciation for those realities that lie on the experiential rather than on the doctrinal side of the theological spectrum. Inspired by Schleiermacher's translation of religion into experience, the emphasis in worship praxis in some churches after 1850 moved from the conceptual to the perceptual. The word "liturgy" began to enter the vocabularies of some Protestant seminaries and their seminarians. While the Civil War was being fought on Piedmont battlefields, the war over liturgy began to be waged in seminaries and churches by those who were for it and those who were against it. Those who were for it were labeled "high church"; those against it, "low church." A new kind of historicism enabled professors and pastors to look more benignly at the thousand years between the patristic period and the Reformation, and they rediscovered some liturgical practices that the prejudices of former generations had forgotten or anathematized.

The architectural consequences of the romantic movement were that stained glass began to replace colonial clear panes, center pulpits were pushed off to the sides, "altars" replaced communion tables and were nailed against the east walls, and worship took on a linear perspective colored more often by aesthetic than liturgical motivations. Whereas the colonial-period churches often were configured for congregational seating around the pulpit, which often was on the long wall, by the late nineteenth century church naves were getting longer, narrower, darker, and more European in their furnishings. Chancels sometimes were added to extend the meeting rooms, and pews were reconfigured perpendicular to the long wall to fit aesthetically the stretched-out space. Especially during the church-building boom following World War II, many sanctuaries were built or renovated according to what the prevailing architectural fashion called "altar-centered," that is, with the altar or table against the back wall. Preachers began to appear in ecclesiastical attire, depending on how much was tolerated by denominational and congregational canons of appropriateness, and sometimes they even oriented their prayers toward the back-wall altars. Choirs, too, were vested and were divided by cathedral-like chancels across which both choirs sang and organ pipes spoke at each other without the acknowledgment that there was a congregation gathered somewhere at the other end of the building. The goal was the creation of a "church-y" feel and look.

The vernacularization of the mass by the Second Vatican Council in the 1960s spilled over into Protestantism. Protestant liturgical scholarship rediscovered that eucharist is not an occasional appendage to the worship service but integral to each Sunday's celebration of Word and Sacrament. Roman Catholic priests all at once found themselves needing to preach and sometimes asked their Protestant clergy friends if they could borrow commentaries on the Scriptures, some of which were known to have exceeded their shelf-life and were layered with decades of dust! The liturgies on both sides began to reveal that the ecumenical church had recovered an understanding of the unity of the Word read from the Bible and preached from the pulpit. Clergy and congregations were surprised to find that in some of the denominationally sanctioned liturgies the sermon got pushed early in the order of things, right after the reading of Scripture.

Accompanying the liturgical activity that produced a plethora of new denominational prayer books, library shelves of alternative and experimental liturgies also were printed in all sizes, shapes, and colors. "Relevant" was the catchword of the 1970s, and it was felt by many that even the new denominational liturgies had not taken the liturgical revolution far enough to enable worship to be relevant to a generation labeled "flower children." One Pennsylvania church began to advertise its early service on Sunday as "relevant worship" and prompted some of us to ask whether the second service therefore was "irrelevant"! Other churches began advertising "contemporary" worship services utilizing alternative musical styles and liturgical expressions that in more recent times have been adapted and canonized by the church-growth movement. Worship leaders began to be bombarded with all sorts of new liturgical materials designed to make the Sunday morning experience more appealing to a rebellious generation that had little love for tradition. Paperback collections of new songs and prayers appeared in all sorts of strange sizes and colors. Some congregations published — frequently without securing copyright permission — their own three-ring-binder alternative hymnals. One pastor neighbor, overwhelmed with the flood of new resources, pleadingly asked me over the backyard fence, "But how do I put it all together?"

Although the liturgical renewal movement had discovered the unity of Word and Sacrament, sermons based on old assumptions often were simply inserted into the slots the new orders of worship assigned. Then in 1971 an obscure professor of Bible in a small southwestern seminary published a book titled *As One without Authority.* In the introduction to this small volume Fred Craddock asks, "The Bible is rich in forms of expression,...whereas most sermons, which seek to communicate the messages of that treasury of materials, are all essentially the same form. Why should...the multitude of needs in the congregation be brought together in one unvarying mold, and that copied from Greek rhetoricians of centuries ago?"[3] Craddock's call for a turnaround in preaching was the harbinger of a larger renaissance in preaching that has been occurring ever since and that has opened the way, I maintain, to some new approaches to crafting and doing liturgy as well.

For centuries preaching in the Western world had been premised on Enlightenment understandings of human reason, that is, on "marshaling an argument in logical sequence, coordinating and subordinating points by the canons of logic, all in a careful appeal to the reasonable hearer."[4] Today, when information is readily accessible electronically in the privacy of one's own Internet browser, "hearer" may be transformed into "reader." Professor Gail Ramshaw muses in her introductory textbook for the study of Christian worship, "If religion is largely information, then we can access it without having to assemble with others on Sunday, and much in our society suggests that information is the road we must take to reach what is good."[5] If the religious quest is perceived merely as the private pursuit of information, then it is still captive to the same rationalism that scissored much of the New Testament from Thomas Jefferson's Bible and reduced much of mainline American Protestant worship to exercises in positive thinking and lectures in right living.

The work begun by Craddock and continued by others has been to wean preachers away from trying to deduce the truth of God by rational argumentation, to an inductive approach uniting both the form and the content of the sermon and centering on the listeners' (plural and corporate) experience of the Scriptures. Gail O'Day writes,

> Preachers readily turn to Scripture for the subject of sermons, but that is not enough. The Bible offers much more than the subject matter for preaching. Preachers also need to turn to Scripture for the decisive, shaping language of sermons.... To preach the gospel, we must know and be shaped by the primary language of our faith. We must enter into the language of Scripture, listen to what and how that language speaks about God and our relationship to God. We must listen to how the Bible itself proclaims the gospel and allow our preaching to be reshaped by the Bible's preaching.... I want preachers to think about the Bible not as a source to be mined for its content, but as a model that can provide both warrants and metaphors for what preachers do.[6]

The task of the preacher as interpreter, Craddock explains, "is not to transform, explain, apply, or otherwise build bridges from the text to the listeners. Rather, the task is to release the text upon the listener's ear by translating it into the language of the listener."[7] "It will be true," Barbara Brown Taylor affirms, "not at the level of explanation but at the level of experience."[8] She continues,

> There is another way to preach, in which the preacher addresses the congregation not as mute students but as active partners in the process of discovering God's word. The sermon traces the preacher's own process of discovery, inviting the congregation to come along and providing them with everything they need to make their own finds. The movement of the sermon...finally leads both preacher and congregation into the presence of God, a place that cannot be explained but only experienced.[9]

Fred Craddock, Barbara Brown Taylor, James Forbes, Barbara Lund-blad, and others, both in their discourses about preaching and in their own sermons, prompted me to ponder: Is there another way to do liturgics? Can the same mode of inductive interpretation in the creating of sermons also inform the crafting of liturgy in the shape of Scripture? Can the same process that leads toward an assembly's encounter with the Word of God in the sermon also enable them to experience God's presence throughout the whole of the worship event? Is there a way that the discoveries in the field of homiletics also can inform the tasks about which liturgics are concerned so that the two disciplines, often seen as separate and even warring against each other, can be brought together in the common task that worship leaders face each week in the preparation for worship? These questions initiate the conversation that is the subject of this book.

Scripture as the Text of Worship

The primary texts that are the concern of homiletics and liturgics are not just any old texts from the classics in literature nor from the most up-to-date list of best sellers nor from the codex that the latest "ism" has declared to be politically correct. The source-texts for worship and preaching are those texts canonized as *the* Scriptures in the sixty-six books of the Old and New Testaments. One seminary professor was asked by a student, "But why must I preach on the Bible?" Apparently the student either was absent from the church history class when the Reformation concept of *sola scriptura* was discussed or had not yet encountered Professor John Burgess's definitive treatise *Why Scripture Matters*.[10] The texts that confront us are the texts of Scripture that the community has accepted as the *regula fidei*,[11] and the presupposition is that *these* texts will become the source for this encounter with the Word of God in the community's worship conversation with the texts. Throughout the history of the Christian experience there have been unresolved debates over what books should be included in or excluded from the canon. Depending on which doctrinal and/or ecclesiological camp a certain tradition within the church finds itself, the counting of canonical books varies. To enable the church to deal with the historical and ecumenical tension over the canon, Burgess provides the following advice:

> We are not free to alter the canon on our own; any alteration must be a confessional act of the church. But [at the same time] we must always be open to the possibility that we have misjudged which writings truly set forth Christ. God's self-revelation is larger than our efforts to define it canonically.[12]

Obviously in the community's liturgical actions these canonical texts will be juxtaposed with other texts — hymns, homilies, prayers, and other verbal and nonverbal expressions. Yet the normative and definitive texts will be those of Holy Scripture. The Scottish tradition of the "beadle" who carries the Bible to the pulpit at the beginning of worship is a nonverbal way of declaring which texts the church considers holy and therefore will be opened for this communal conversation with the Word of God.

The Bible cannot exist in isolation from the community of interpretation that engages itself with the biblical texts. Scriptures separated from the church, as Stanley Hauerwas rightly has said, ironically becomes "the seedbed of fundamentalism, as well as biblical criticism."[13] Burgess comments:

> People on each side of one controversial issue or another turn to Scripture to support a position, after they have already made up their minds. The tendency to read Scripture as information reinforces this attitude. We go to the text, looking for those pieces of information that will support our particular cause. We reduce texts with layers of meaning to one "right meaning." We then reject this meaning,

arguing that it is historically conditioned (and therefore irrelevant to our situation), or appeal to it as an authoritative word that should settle the debate once and for all.[14]

Seeking to find an alternative way of approaching the Bible that enables the church to get beyond the polarities that the cultural wars have spawned he proposes:

> Scripture is more than revealed truths about God and is more than a language, however profound, for describing the heights and depths of the human condition. Rather, Scripture is a sacramental word that points beyond itself. . . . When Scripture is read, when it is explicated in preaching, when it is incorporated into prayers of thanksgiving and lament, when it frames the celebration of the Lord's Supper, Scripture becomes a means by which Christians are gathered into the body of the living Lord.[15]

Burgess's idea of Scripture as "sacramental Word"[16] is akin to the perspective that informs the following pages of this discussion. Scripture matters, but, again in Burgess's words: "what makes Scripture *Scripture* is its capacity to mediate an encounter with the transcendent."[17] This theme will reemerge in the next chapter in greater detail.

We live in a time of biblical illiteracy in the pews and, unfortunately, sometimes also in pulpits. Seminary professors and ecclesiastical committees charged with the nurture and examination of candidates for ordination continually bemoan students' lack of basic knowledge of the church's basic book, the Bible. In an atmosphere of relative and multiple authorities many lay and clergy alike have been given license to base their faith definitions and their ethical judgments and actions on human experience without any understanding or desire to explore what Walter Brueggemann calls "the counterworld of evangelical imagination"[18] that informs Scripture and tradition. Mandatory courses in Bible and church history often are things to be endured by seminarians so that they can get on to the more exciting stuff that each individual finds more self-fulfilling. Seekers, many times with little or no prior exposure or involvement in faith communities yet trying to recover from the addictions into which a secular culture has lured them, search to "find" themselves amid the jungle of cultural life-options and enroll in seminaries to try to discover their vocation.

Yet too many graduate without the elementary skills in Bible, history, and theology to become the learned leaders in the church that most Christian faith traditions revere and most congregations expect. These gaps in the training of leaders appear most perceptibly — and this is my confessed prejudice — in the skills necessary for the leadership of public worship that is at the center of a congregation's life. In the curricula of many seminaries students can fulfill a practical theology requirement through the successful completion of a course in preaching; yet little or no attention is given to the formation of *liturgical* leaders, except when required by ecclesiastical judicatories or ordaining bodies. Hopefully, this small volume may be of assistance not only to those regularly charged with the responsibility for planning and leading worship but also particularly to those preparing for the awesome office of Word and Sacrament that accompanies the call of Jesus Christ to various forms of ministry.

Amid an increasing curiosity regarding things spiritual in our culture, there is also a growing interest in biblical studies and a yearning to encounter in worship this special God in Christ to whom the Bible points. Particularly we see this searching among those either entering faith communities for the first time or reentering after an exile. Hopefully these newly initiated, together with those reared in the faith, will encounter in worship — and rarely today is there any other corporate setting for exposure to Scripture — what one theologian years ago called "the strange new world of the Bible." And as they are engaged by those ancient words that shape the church's worship, they hopefully will experience the one Word, Jesus Christ, and find their lives shaped by him.

Choosing the Texts

How from the thousands of texts in the Bible will the specific text(s) for a particular worship service be chosen? At the occasion of Jesus' first sermon (Luke 4:16ff.) he "was given" a scriptural passage to read, namely, the text of Isaiah 61:1–2. Two methods of providing for the objective "given-ness" of texts for proclamation have arisen in the church's life. One is a lectionary of selected readings based on the seasons and festivals of the church. Another is what is known as *lectio continua,* or continuous reading of Scripture, that is, each Sunday's texts pick up where last Sunday's ended. Either method pushes the community's conversation with the Word away from the subjectivity of the preacher's pet texts and peeves.

And for most of the Christian experience the church, with historic precedence in Judaism, has relied on either or a combination of these two methods to choose scripture texts for worship.

Although the interpreter's preunderstanding of the text(s) is unavoidable and is an integral part of the interpretive process, the discipline of following a lectionary for preaching and worship forces the preacher and the community to be engaged by texts which they themselves would not choose. A lectionary moves the Bible in corporate worship from an object of the preacher's own manipulation — sometimes literally *in the hand* — to become the source from which the community's common worship emerges. Hence, the Bible from which the texts are read in worship should be too big a book to be handled comfortably by reader, preacher, or parishioner. It rests, rather, on a pulpit or ambo where it is opened as part of the community's liturgical action. In some traditions a separate Book of the Gospels is carried into the midst of the assembly, where the Gospel lection for the day is read. The Bible, even when the Gospel is read from a separate book, is the church's book, and a lectionary helps the whole church focus on the common texts that not only shape its worship life, but also can organize its programs of education, the arts and music, and its stewardship and outreach. Despite the reality that there can be no ultimate objectivity in approaching the text(s), allowing a lectionary to choose the texts is one measure of protection against the subjectivity that has characterized much of Protestant worship. The lens the lectionary provides focuses the community on a corporate *engagement* with a text that comes from beyond itself rather than on the random *selection* of a text according to the likes and dislikes of the worship leader. *A Three-Year Banquet: The Lectionary for the Assembly,* by Professor Gail Ramshaw, is a wonderful tool to help congregations understand the importance of a lectionary in corporate worship.[19]

The work of the ecumenical Consultation on Common Texts that originated in the mid-1960s among many denominations, including Roman Catholics in the United States and Canada, has had a significant impact on worship and preaching in the last decades. Their work has produced contemporary English texts for the Lord's Prayer, the classic creeds, and canticles held in common among the participating churches. These ecumenical texts are the ones that I have used in the liturgical expressions and musical settings in this book. The most monumental accomplishment of the Consultation was the *Common Lectionary,* reworked and published in

1992 as the *Revised Common Lectionary*. This calendar of readings from the Scriptures on a three-year cycle is based on the Roman Catholic *Lectionary for Mass* of 1969. It has been adopted by most mainline Protestant denominations in the United States and Canada and has been included in their prayer books, hymnals, and, in some cases, in yearly desk calendars published by denominational agencies.

The *Revised Common Lectionary* combines the concept of special readings for the seasons and festivals during the first part of the church year from Advent to Pentecost with an alternate modified *lectio continua* ordering during the season after Pentecost. The texts from the Old Testament, Epistles, Gospels, and Psalms for the first semester of the church year from Advent through the festival of Pentecost are selected for their appropriateness to the seasons and festivals, some of which are determined by when Easter falls. Hence the number of Sundays in the season of Epiphany varies.

During the second semester, the season of Pentecost, the lections after the first Sunday are called "propers" and are scheduled for specific Sundays according to the secular calendar, for example, June 18, June 25. Thus, depending on when Pentecost falls (determined, of course, by Easter) in any given year, some of the propers will not be part of the lectionary for that year. The propers generally are selections of Old Testament, Epistle, and Gospel texts that follow in the order in which these texts appear in the various biblical books, although one Sunday's lections may not be contiguous to those of the preceding Sunday. In Year B, for example, the Epistle Proper for the Sunday between August 14 and August 20 inclusive (Proper 15) is Ephesians 5:15–20, while on the next Sunday Proper 16 is Ephesians 6:10–20. Thematic connections between the four texts is more intentional during the first semester from Advent to Pentecost than in the second semester after Pentecost.

The *Revised Common Lectionary* has received incredibly wide acceptance and use in the ecumenical community. Interdenominational Bible study groups bring local clusters of pastors together to read and study the texts that will be the basis for their preaching. The same texts are read simultaneously in churches across denominational barriers and traditions creating a sense of unity around the Scriptures. One woman who was part of a weekly study of the texts in one of the congregations I served as pastor accompanied a group of confirmands to the National Cathedral in

Washington, D.C. As the lector began reading the Old Testament Lesson, she leaned over to me and said somewhat astonished, "That's the same Bible passage we studied on Tuesday!" The *Common Lectionary* has become a unifying center that has enabled individual congregations to see themselves as parts of a bigger church.

The lectionary also has been a primary help in the integration of the homiletical and liturgical disciplines. Worship leaders and interested lay persons in many congregations and parishes gather weekly around the lectionary to read and study the texts that will be part of their common worship life. Parish musicians select music according to the lectionary. One denominationally produced hymnal contains an index listing hymns appropriate for each of the Sundays and festivals in the three-year cycle of the *Revised Common Lectionary*.[20] Teams of musicians and theologians have composed volumes of new hymns, both music and words, specifically to accompany the texts of the lectionary. Poets and pastors have published volumes of prayers, litanies, and other worship resources based on the lections for each Sunday in the three-year cycle. Denominational educational ministries and interdenominational publishing houses have created curricula oriented around the lectionary readings in the attempt to integrate worship and Christian education. Bulletin covers published by denominational offices and private entrepreneurs feature artwork and interpretive materials coordinated with the lectionary readings.

From Lectionary to Liturgy

In short, the *Common Lectionary* and its revision have focused the whole church's attention on the biblical texts themselves and have freed preaching and worship from the subjectivities that inevitably arise when the worship leadership picks and chooses texts to fit preconceived themes or prejudices. It has brought into a common conversation around the texts what formerly were isolated voices concerned with their own agendas. As I move from congregation to congregation each week I find, at least in my setting of pastoral responsibility, an almost universal use of the lectionary. Is there a way, I began to ask myself, that the lectionary, as it has reshaped the practice of preaching, also can inform the whole of the worship experience so that the liturgical action itself is shaped by the scripture texts to which the lectionary points in the yearly drama of God's saving work in Christ?

My pastor neighbor's question, "How do I put it all together?" prompted my earlier work, *Worship Vessels: Resources for Renewal,* in which I presented some of the worship resources I had crafted along with some brief rationales and rubrics for their use in worship.[21] Essentially that volume, which generally is shelved under "liturgics," was a collection of prayers, litanies, and orders for baptism, eucharist, marriage, and burial, with some hints at how my pastor neighbor and others might put those expressions together in the crafting of liturgies. That collection subsequently has been revised and enlarged into a two-volume set, one for services of Word and Sacrament, *Immersed in the Splendor of God: Resources for Worship Renewal,*[22] and its companion, *Blessed by the Presence of God: Liturgies for Occasional Services.*[23]

This book takes my neighbor's question on a different route. I hope that what is here still is focused on the praxis of ministry and that it may effect some practical changes in worship practice. Yet my primary goal here is not to provide the resources for worship renewal but to engage worship leaders themselves in the process of crafting the expressions that may be appropriate in their own particular worship settings and to integrate preaching and liturgy so that no longer, to use Professor Charles Rice's wonderful image, will the sermon be "a kind of homiletical ocean liner preceded by a few liturgical tugboats."[24] So I ask: Is there a shared hermeneutic that will forge homiletics and liturgics into a common pursuit? Is there a common approach to worship that will change the greetings following the service on Sundays from "Good sermon, Reverend," to "Wow, everything came together today!"? The pursuit of whatever it is that can bring it all together is the subject of this excursion into the process that leads from lectionary to liturgy and the crafting of worship in the shape of Scripture.

TWO

Engaging the Scriptures

Despite the revolution in liturgics and the renaissance in preaching that occurred during the latter part of the twentieth century, there still lingers in much of Protestantism the liturgical model left over from revivalism in which the sermon is considered to be the climax of the service. And the possibility still remains that the renewed interest in preaching today, because it is the fruit of work in the homiletical disciplines, will continue to foster this liturgical aberration. Ocean-liner sermons preceded by some liturgical tugboats have not been rendered obsolete by the space-age multimedia "messages" of the megachurch movement! Yet many of the worship resources being produced by denominations and independent authors today still reflect the underlying rationalism of the nineteenth century that continues to inform the so-called "contemporary" worship practices that many churches feel they need to employ to attract more people in the twenty-first century. In an insightful essay, "Re-Assembly: Participation as Faith Construction," Professor Melinda Quivik warns, "...worship conducted for an ulterior purpose — for something other than worship — is worship that has gone astray. If worship does not intend to be significant in the present, it has lost is point, its center."[1]

Liturgy as Proclamation

Contrary to the continuing tenacity of the nineteenth-century understandings, there is theological, historical, and practical evidence to demonstrate that a sermon is only one act within *a corporate liturgical action that in its entirety intends to become a proclamatory event in which the Word of God is enacted and experienced.* This approach, which may appear somewhat radical to some, is premised on the thesis that not only does preaching take place in a liturgical context, but also the *whole liturgical action itself becomes a proclamatory event.* Liturgical and homiletical scholars very rarely want to expand the definition of proclamation to include the whole worship event. Roman Catholic liturgical scholar William Skudlarek made the passing suggestion nearly three decades ago that "it is also possible . . . to interpret liturgy as a form of proclamation, and preaching as a form of worship."[2] Yet he proceeds by developing the second alternative, namely, preaching as a form of worship rather than the whole liturgical action as a form of proclamation.

In a small article by Gordon Lathrop buried in an anthology of readings on liturgy produced by the Liturgical Conference, he concludes: "The whole liturgy, this whole pattern of juxtaposed 'words,' says the faith of the church and the truth of God. The whole liturgy proclaims."[3] Proclamation of God's good news is more than the delivery of a sermon, more than the arrival of a newspaper on a strange doorstep under the cover of night. Proclamation that is the engagement of a biblical text with a worshiping community occurs throughout the liturgical interaction of the community in its conversation with God. All aspects of the worship experience from gathering to sending, including sermon and sacraments, are interrelated parts of a unified engagement with the Scriptures and a unified enactment of the Word of God.

Patricia Wilson-Kastner agreed that "sermons are not interruptions of the liturgy but integral parts thereof."[4] Yet her starting point was a given ritual into which a sermon is integrated. I want to begin from the opposite pole, namely, that the whole worship service is a Word event and that a sermon is but one expression of the Word being embodied in a unified corporate liturgical action. Paul Scott Wilson maintains:

> Preaching takes place in the context of worship. Something so obvious need scarcely be said, except that the implications are often overlooked. This means that the sermon or homily does not bear the entire weight of God's Word. God speaks through the prayers and hymns and all aspects of the service, *but speaks in a particular and indispensable way* [emphasis added] in the opening up of the scripture for today and in the breaking of bread and the drinking of wine.[5]

Is limiting preaching as a means of grace to sermon and sacrament a restriction that needs a second look? The implications certainly often *are* overlooked, and it is my intention in this book to explore the processes and the results if *all* parts of the service are conceptualized as aspects of one enactment of the Word of God. Homiletics and liturgics are integrally related disciplines that coalesce in this unified event, and in the praxis of ministry the responsibilities of homilist and liturgist are integral to each other and inseparable from each other. They get in the act together.

Integrating Homiletics and Liturgics

Homiletics, traditionally defined as the art of preaching, finds its origin in the Greek *homiletike*, the art of conversing. Preaching is a conversation (*homilia*) — generally spoken (oral) and meant to be heard (aural) in the context of an assembly and embedded within a corporate liturgical action. Yet the intention of this conversation is to be in communion with realities greater than itself. Or, put another way, the words of the human conversation mean to be the mode by which the divine Word is enacted and heard. The conversation is not just *about* God but is *with* God. The engagement is with a biblical text, but with the intention that God whose Word is witnessed to in the text will engage us now with the Word of judgment and grace. So ultimately the conversationalist in the conversation is One other than the person identified as the preacher. The homiletic intention ultimately is for the conversation with the text and with the community to become so transparent that God emerges as the conversationalist engaging in a conversation with the people of God.

The root of these words is the Greek word *homilos* which, translated literally, is "crowd." Homiletics presupposes a crowd, but a special crowd that in Scripture and tradition is called "church," literally the ones "called out." Although events like evangelistic gatherings in sports arenas and electronically recorded audio and video broadcasts may include discourses, the intended context for the conversation is that special crowd we call the church. And by "church" I do not mean only an assembly gathered in a certain time and place for worship but also the church in all its wider missional settings and the church as the whole communion of saints with whom we are in historic community and continuity in time and beyond time.

In the introduction to his unique work on ecclesiology from a liturgical perspective, Gordon Lathrop begins *Holy People,* with a chapter on "Assembly." "Assembly, a gathering together of participating persons," he maintains

> constitutes the most basic symbol of Christian worship. All the other symbols and symbolic actions of liturgy depend upon this gathering being there in the first place. No texts are read, no preaching occurs, no hymns are sung, no eucharist is held without an assembly, however small or large this gathering of persons may be.[6]

American Christianity tends to identify "church" as a place for worship, and, with a bit of catechizing, as the people who worship in that place. Perhaps "assembly" may be a more precise word to describe this special gathering of people in a certain location who claim the texts as Holy Scripture and who wait for God's Word to be heard again. Nevertheless, I also want to see "church" as more than an insular congregation defined by its four walls and organizational structure.

Regardless of the denominational label or ecclesiastical polity, most American Protestants are functional congregationalists. They conceive of "church" as "congregation." And worship generally is perceived as that which takes place in particular congregations. By the way, the root of "congregation" comes from the Latin word for "herd," yes, "herd" as of elephants and tigers and other mammalian species. There are some who might push the metaphor a bit further depending on their experience with certain herds. Yet, as I have discovered first hand in my work, there are wider settings of "church" where proclamation also takes place. If it were not so, then my office would be that of a director of a not-for-profit corporation, and my speakings would be nothing more than fund-raising talks. The soil in which the Word of God grows is implanted and bears fruit is the *homilos,* the community, the assembly, the church, that special group in congregational and wider settings that God has called out and herded together, and without which there would be no *homilia,* no conversation, and no reason for this book.

The *homilia*, therefore, is a communal conversation. Because of the lack of an identifiable plural "you" in English, coupled with a long-standing and an ever-increasing spirit of individualism in American culture, there is a danger of overhearing the Bible's "you" as singular. Yet the grammars of the Hebrew and Greek Testaments are quite clear: God's "you" is a plural "you." In a footnote Gordon Lathrop makes an interesting observation:

> Even *Philemon,* which seems at first to be a letter to one individual, includes other names as well as "the church in your house" ... in its address. Its opening and closing greeting (verse 3 and 25), echoing a communal liturgical setting are addressed to a plural *you.* The letter presumes a public reading and a community that will assist and witness the response of the individual.[7]

Indeed, there are times of retreat when each person, at Jesus' invitation, needs to go into the privacy of his or her own prayer chamber, shut the door, and pray (Matt. 6:6). Yet the notion of private spirituality is a contradiction in terms, for although the Holy Spirit descends on individuals, as Jesus experienced in his baptism, and gives individual gifts, the Spirit that blew through the house where all were sitting on Pentecost and the Spirit that is promised "to you and your children and to all who are far off" is a community-creating Spirit. We can know God only because God's previous conversations with the community have been passed on in the community. Thus, there cannot be a conversation with the texts without the community, and it is a conversation that cannot be without the Homilist who initiates the conversation. Homiletics is about *God's* conversation with the people of God.

The common equation of "preaching" with "sermonizing" has restricted us from a far richer and more integrative understanding of the proclamation of the Word. Interestingly, the verb "preach" occurs only three times in the New Revised Standard Version of the New Testament, while in the King James Version "preach" (translated from any one of three verbs: *kerussein, euaggelizein,* and *kataggellein*) occurs over a hundred times. The NRSV translates the same three Greek verbs as "proclaim." Likewise, *kerugma,* the noun form of *kerussein,* which in the KJV was rendered as "preaching," in the NRSV becomes "proclamation." Could it be that this shift from preaching to proclamation is a result of an increasing narrowing of "preaching" to "sermonizing" that has taken place over the past four hundred years? Could it be that "preaching" has accumulated some negative overtones that make "proclamation" a more acceptable translation?

My point for such an excursion into New Testament Greek is that "preaching" or "proclamation" needs to be expanded into a wider experience of the Word of God than that which is generally labeled "sermon." Henceforth in this discussion I shall use the more inclusive term "proclamation" to identify the encounter with the Word of God that occurs throughout the worship service. Doran and Troeger report that "recent scholarship in 'performance studies' suggests that [in the early church] the gospel may have been proclaimed in a number of dramatic and oratorical forms."[8] When we survey the myriad of settings and situations in which proclamation in the Scriptures took place, we are opened to a far wider understanding of what is encompassed in the whole proclamation event. We discover also, as we shall explore in depth later, that the Scriptures themselves point to a liturgical action, that is, to a progression of interrelated actions that form a unified experience as God is in conversation with the people of God.

Let it be said in more than a footnote that the restriction of "preaching" to "sermon" may be the result of certain biases on the part of those to whom preaching traditionally has been entrusted. The idea that the sermon is the central focus of the worship experience and that everything else in the service is simply an opening exercise is an assumption that sometimes may be arrived at more by the ones in pulpits than the ones in pews!

While I was actively engaged in parish ministry in Colorado, despite my aversion to doing sociological studies in worship, I conducted a series of surveys as part of another study to gather worshipers' perceptions regarding which of the various parts and expressions in a worship service enabled them to be brought into an encounter with God. I envisioned this not as a statistical survey that would yield measurable results. Rather, the intent was more to gather perceptual reactions. The atmosphere for any survey of people's attitudes toward worship is not a sterile laboratory but a sanctuary sanctified and set apart for the enactment of a congregation's sacred story. The subjects were not a cross section of the population but a congregation of people who had made a previous commitment to the church community and had other reasons for coming to worship than to participate in a research survey. There were no control groups, no placebos, no random samplings. Any conclusions about people's perceptions always are colored by the realization that such surveys try to measure, at the least, a highly subjective subject, and, at the most, intrude on the nonsensory realms of a congregation's deepest spirituality. The results, however, were truly enlightening, especially the unsolicited anecdotal comments that people appended to the questions. Through which worship expressions did those who participated in these surveys in this church perceive they were brought into an encounter with God?

It became quite clear, even after the first Sunday's survey, that a significant percentage of that worshiping community, despite age and sex differences, perceived that the other worship acts were just as helpful as the sermon, sometimes even more so, in engaging them in the worship of God. Different people indicated that they entered into the encounter with God through a variety of worship acts and expressions. Further, there was no unanimity as to which ones were more helpful than the others. One woman wrote at the end of her bulletin: "All acts help me to worship. I would not like to do without any of them." To some people, even the sanctuary setting provided more engagement with God than the sermon. What I had gathered for the first time was a set of data and a collection of anecdotal reflections that substantiated what for years I had held in theory, namely, that proclamation occurs through each act and throughout the whole of the worship experience and that some people find certain acts more helpful in engaging them in the preaching event than others. Now if anyone wants to claim that the sermon is still the only thing that people come for in worship, at least I can refer to a study in one mainline Protestant congregation that indicated otherwise!

But was this merely an isolated survey that had no correlation with what happens in other churches? My findings had been the results of worshipers' perceptions in one congregation where I was the crafter of the liturgies and the worship leader. What would happen, I wondered, if the same surveys were conducted in other congregations with other leaders in another geographic location? A year later I enlisted a group of five parish clergy in Pennsylvania and asked them to conduct the same surveys on the same two Sundays in the congregations they served. Each of them provided the same questionnaires in the bulletins on the appointed Sundays and provided me with the results together with their own anecdotal analyses and findings.

Interestingly, but not surprisingly, the results were almost identical to what had happened in another congregation seventeen hundred miles away a year earlier. Again, not one particular worship act was perceived to be more helpful than the others. In other words, the sermon was not more important to people than the other worship acts, and in some instances people in all five churches, on Sundays when the eucharist was celebrated, perceived the communion as more important than the sermon. One pastor analyzed the results in her congregation: "Communion was first, the sermon second, and the scripture readings third." Another said, "I came to these sessions believing that the sermon is the most important part of the service. I have had my eyes opened."

Since the eucharist was deemed so helpful, one pastor wondered why there was such reticence to increasing the frequency of communion. Another pastor was "shocked" that the offertory was an important way of encountering God to so many people — a comment echoed by one of her colleagues. He added that he also "never anticipated that the penitential act was as important [to people] as it was [according to survey results]." One pastor, assessing the result of the survey in her congregation, concluded, "The people taught me that everything is sacred." As they listened to the reports of each other's findings, one pastor said, "We all did the same thing in five different congregations, yet the results were all the same." One is led to wondering whether, if the same survey were replicated in other mainline Protestant worshiping congregations, the same findings would emerge. I am willing to wager that the consensus would be a "yes."

Worship as Event

These views from the pews tell us that people's perception of what helps them be engaged by the Word of God is more encyclopedic in scope than what those of us who have been trained as preachers sometimes imagine. Worshipers experience the total worship service as an event in which something happens — happens to them individually and happens to the corporate community as God meets them in this event. Is asking people, as we did in the survey questions, to "indicate to what extent the acts of worship helped you to worship God in the service today" not another way of asking them what they perceive to be the means of grace? Is enabling people to be in touch with realities greater than themselves not what John the Baptist came to preach in the wilderness and Jesus came from his baptism in the Jordan and his temptation in the desert to proclaim? And are not the acts in which people experience the nearness of the realm of God as varied, yet just as efficacious, as a cleansing bath to claim one for a new life and a prophetic word spoken to change the heart and a eucharistic bread to nourish the soul and a sacramental touch to heal the body?

Although the Reformation of the sixteenth century effected a diminution in the number of sacraments, at the same time the reformers expanded the idea of what a sacrament is. To Luther there ultimately was only one Sacrament — Jesus Christ — with whom the believer is joined and signed by God in baptism, preaching, and the eucharist. To Calvin the Word read aloud from Scripture and preached in the sermon was "one liturgical act" conveying the incarnate Word and a "sign" through which Jesus Christ approaches people and effects his claim on them.[9] The realization that Christ comes to us in both Sacrament *and* Word was the overwhelming discovery of the Reformation in the sixteenth century and of the Second Vatican Council in the twentieth. "Word" is not the words of ancient writ alone, just as "sacrament" is not just some mechanical ritual of remembrance. "Word" and "Sacrament," together with all the other rich verbal and visual components accompanying those signs, are the event in which Jesus the Word is enfleshed again in the community of faith. Everything, including sermon and sacraments, is Word enacted. Everything in corporate worship is Word, because what worship is about ultimately is encountering Jesus the Word.

And how does Word witnessed to in words of a different time and different place and among different people of different languages become Word for a worshiping community today? Forty-five years ago I underlined some words of Gerhard Ebeling in a book that even now wants to fall open to those lines: "Whatever precise theological definition may be given to the *concept of the Word of God*, at all events it points us to something that happens...."[10] One of the problems in translation is that the verb "to happen" in German is *geschehen,* but in the noun form *Geschehen* is translated "event." The Word of God is an event. The Word of God happens.

Yet for the event to take place, something else needs to be engaged. Professor Ebeling's sentence goes on, and my underlining continues: "...*viz.* to the movement which leads from the text of holy scripture to the sermon ('sermon' of course taken in the pregnant sense of proclamation in general)."[11] Something happens in that movement from the text of Holy Scripture to whatever mode of proclamation in the worship event becomes a vessel through which the Word of God is experienced. Understanding again that his use of *Predigt* in German (translated in English as "sermon") refers literally to "that which is preached," we listen in again to Ebeling:

> The process from text to sermon can...be characterized by saying: proclamation that has taken place is to become proclamation that takes place. This transition from text to sermon is a transition from scripture to the spoken word. Thus the task...consists in making what is written into spoken word or...in letting the text become God's Word again....The movement from text to the sermon is a hermeneutic process....
>
> The sermon as a sermon is not exposition of the text as past proclamation, but is itself proclamation in the present — and that means, then, that the sermon is *execution* of the text. It carries into execution the aim of the text. It is proclamation of what the text has proclaimed. And with that the hermeneutic sense of direction is so to speak reversed. The text which has attained understanding in the exposition now helps to bring to understanding what is to attain understanding by means of the sermon....Thus the text by means of the sermon becomes a hermeneutic aid in the understanding of present experience. Where that happens radically, there true word is uttered, and that in fact means God's Word.[12]

Pardon my abbreviation of some lengthy Germanic-structured sentences, but my intention here is to document that the work that leads to proclamation includes the task of interpretation; homiletics and liturgics are dependent on hermeneutics.

The Role of Interpretation

This is not the place for a protracted elaboration of the intricacies of hermeneutical principles. Let it suffice to say that in the process of interpreting scripture texts so as to allow the Word of God to happen again, what has come to be called the "hermeneutical circle" emerges. David Newman explains:

> Interpretation takes place within a movement from the text to our situation and back to the text....The circle comprises both a hermeneutical function of the situation, in affecting how the text will be understood, and a hermeneutical function of the text, in opening up

a new understanding of our situation. It is not enough, therefore, to speak only of interpreting the text. The goal of the text is not to be interpreted, but to interpret us.[13]

Therefore, not only the worship leader and planner is engaged in the task of interpretation, but also the whole gathered assembly is drawn into the hermeneutical circle. Remember, the context for homiletics is the *homilos,* the "crowd," who bring to the proclamatory event preunderstandings — sometimes called "life-texts" — that will be encountered by the Word. These life-texts peculiar to each *homilos* are drawn into the hermeneutical circle as the scripture texts recontextualize themselves in those communities' conversations with the Word of God. Gordon Lathrop speaks of the interactive roles of all the people engaged in the encounter with the Word of God in the Bible as "a continuing community of interpretation."[14]

David Tracy in the epilogue to his update of Robert Grant's *A Short History of the Interpretation of the Bible* concludes: "Interpretation itself is a process best understood on the model of the conversation.... The preunderstanding of the interpreter and the claim to attention of the text meet in that peculiar interaction called a conversation, where the subject matter itself takes over."[15] Interpreting texts liturgically, as one would interpret texts homiletically, I contend, is the intentional act of setting the conversation in a liturgical context in which the worship leader as the community's interpreter (*hermeneus* in Greek) enables the community with its own unique preunderstandings to be engaged by a biblical text in such a way that the Subject of the text — God — takes over, and the Word-event happens.

Generally pastors are the ones on whom the mantle of *hermeneus* is cast and who have the weekly responsibility of crafting what will become the community's liturgical work in worship. However, musicians, as well as other artistic directors and Christian educators, also are engaged in the hermeneutical work. Therefore I choose to use the term "worship leaders" to refer to all who have this primary interpretive task. They generally are also the ones who preside in worship. Worship leaders as crafters of sermon and liturgy carry the life-texts of the community into the engagement with the appointed biblical text and become the interpreters/crafters of the worship vessels in which the conversation is intended to happen.

Interpreting biblical texts liturgically does not mean merely copying the text's words into a bulletin format — although the reading of biblical passages in themselves is a valid liturgical act. Nor is the creation of a liturgy simply a stringing together of a number of biblical passages. Rather, the kind of liturgical crafting I am advocating is an *interpretive* act in which the worship leader as the community's interpreter/crafter enables both the life-texts of the community *and* the biblical texts to engage in conversations that result in new forms of expression. A helpful tool to enable worship leaders to discern and interpret the "texts" of congregational life and activity is the book by Leonora Tubbs Tisdale, *Preaching as Local Theology and Folk Art,* particularly the chapter "Exegeting the Congregation."[16] She comes to this issue as a homiletician; however her methodology is applicable also in the art of crafting liturgy. We shall address the community's interpretive role more in chapter 4.

Earlier hermeneutics that tried to employ rational or historical disciplines sought to strip away the presuppositions of both interpreter and the community to try to get behind the text and to discover some truth or ideas that would remain after the preunderstandings fell away. Current interpretation theory, however, Tracy reports, acknowledges that "no interpreter enters the process of interpretation without some prejudgments."[17] We bring those preunderstandings into an engagement with the texts in which the texts begin to claim serious attention. In this kind of hermeneutical approach, according to Tracy,

> The primary meaning of the text does not lie "behind" it (in the mind of the author, in the original social setting, in the original audience) nor even "in" the text itself. Rather, the meaning of the text lies *in front of* the text — in the now *common* question, the now common subject matter of both text and interpreter.... [Interpreters] employ all the tools of historical criticism and then seek to mediate, translate, interpret the meaning into their present horizon. Interpreters seek...to "fuse the horizon" of the text (the horizon of meaning in front of the text) with our own horizon.[18]

Although Tracy's frame of reference in these explanations is a more general hermeneutical perspective, such an understanding also is operative more specifically in the homiletical and liturgical tasks related to the crafting of worship services. "Meaning" in the context of the present discussion is not a rational deduction on the part of the one crafting sermon and liturgy but the Word of God recontextualizing itself in the liturgical action of the community.

Therefore, the approach of the crafter/interpreter is that of a servant who allows the texts of Holy Scripture to take over so that, through the working of the Holy Spirit, these encounters with the texts may become communal experiences of the presence of God in Christ. "The liturgical purpose," Lathrop reminds us, "is for something to happen in the use of the texts, not for them to function simply as archaic imagery for our current situation."[19] He continues,

> Juxtaposed to this assembly, the texts are understood by the liturgy to have been transformed to speak now the presence of God's grace. In this way, the texts are made to carry us, who have heard the text and been included in its evocations, into this very transformation: God's grace is present in our lives. Texts are read here as if they were the concrete medium for the encounter with God.[20]

Because the primary focus of the worship event is on God, the individual and corporate experiences of the congregation as they are drawn into the hermeneutical conversation with the biblical texts are not determinative, nor do the experiences limit the Word that will be spoken and heard. The purpose of worship is not to legitimate our own experiences, even though they can be proof-texted by references to Scripture. Worship draws us into the experience *of God*. What constitutes the community and the community's conversation is the one Word, Jesus Christ, becoming enfleshed in the body of Christ through the conversation with the Scriptures that occurs in the worship event. Thus, any hermeneutic for proclamation is primarily and ultimately Christological.

When I was a parish pastor, I met weekly with a group of lay persons in the congregation to read together and to study the texts that were appointed for the following Sunday's worship services. In these sessions the life-texts of the group came into dialogue with the scripture texts in a profound way, and I discovered that on the few occasions when the group did not meet, it was more difficult for me to be about the interpretive task of preaching and crafting liturgy. Although some pastors meet regularly with other clergy to study lectionary texts, such collegial study sessions leave the congregation who will be part of the worship event out of the hermeneutical loop.

Now as a Conference Minister my role is to be pastor to pastors, and it is my responsibility to craft the liturgies and to be the preacher and celebrant in monthly services of Word and Sacrament for pastors. In these settings where I am preacher with preachers, the life-texts of parish pastors begin to engage themselves in the hermeneutical circle, and I have discovered that the sermons and liturgies I craft for these events, although they are based on the *Revised Common Lectionary* texts, more and more are colored by the concerns and issues that pastors face in their praxis of ministry. Moreover, when I am invited to preach in a congregation in which that very same text that was part of the pastors' worship experience is appointed by the lectionary, the sermon will take a vastly different shape. The communities are different, and those differences will weave themselves into the interpretive engagement with the texts differently.

Hermeneutics has to do with engaging the Scriptures so that there is a mode for the Word to become Word again. In recent history, as we have seen above, homiletics has been narrowed to the creation and delivery of sermons. The focus of interpretation has been on the engagement of the *preacher* with the texts and on his or her proclamation in the slice of worship called "sermon." Yet for the whole community to be engaged with the Scriptures there needs to be a sequence of individual acts throughout the whole worship event that aim, in their totality, at a *communal* enactment of the Word of God. Conversation is not unidirectional, not simply a solitary voice speaking to a group listening in silence, but dialogical, a mutual exchange in what F. W. Dillistone calls a "speech community."[21]

Liturgics, the art of crafting and doing liturgy, is concerned with the *sequence* of *communal* acts, verbal and nonverbal, that together form and shape the worship event. Liturgics is about how the Word-event is crafted and enacted communally with the aim that ultimately God in Christ through the Holy Spirit will be engaged in conversation with the people of God. "Liturgy" is derived from the Greek *leitourgia* meaning "work" or "service." It is used by the writers of the New Testament to describe what the followers of the Way of Christ *do,* and in the New Testament what is done is always done in a communal setting. A remnant of the original meaning of this multifaceted word is preserved when churches call what happens in their conversation with God a worship "service." Sometimes the sequence of acts is called an "order of worship" or a "liturgy," yet it is important to emphasize that a liturgy is not what is printed in a prayer book or a worship flier but what *happens* when a community is doing its work of worshiping God.

Rarely a title or position is given to one who spends his or her life studying and practicing the art of liturgics. However, at least one of the giants in the field of liturgics in the twentieth century labeled such a person a "liturgiologist."[22] Liturgiologists sometimes have tended to the art as one would to the curatorship of an ancient shrine rather than to the sustenance of the clients who frequent the shrine. Some of us liturgiologists at times have liked to amuse ourselves with rearranging the furniture in the shrine, ensuring that such arrangements are according to ancient codes of furniture arrangement and guaranteeing that when the clients gather they use the furniture properly. Those of us who dabble in things liturgical have tended to do our own thing with those "other" things that happen in worship while we have left homiletical things — that is, sermon-things — to the homileticians.

Gregory Dix's classic analysis, *The Shape of the Liturgy,* has virtually nothing at all to say about the proclamation of the Word.[23] He devotes the equivalent of 2 pages out of 764 to the role of the sermon. And although the economies of seminaries have tended to force the offices of those who teach homiletics and liturgics into one person, often that one person's interests and expertises in one or the other discipline have overshadowed and even excluded the other. Yet homiletics and liturgics are both about proclamation, and it is my contention that as a worship leader looks to next Sunday, he or she is both a homiletician and liturgiologist simultaneously whether or not the church has enough in the budget to pay for two people to look together at next Sunday's service!

Homiletics and liturgics, I contend, are wedded together in the proclamation event because both share a common hermeneutical process as the Scriptures are recontextualized in the community's conversation with God in Christ through the Holy Spirit. Both disciplines are employed together to craft for the community what happens in the community's encounter with the Word of God. Volumes have been written concerning the interpretation of texts in preaching, yet precious little has been said about a *liturgical hermeneutic.* My thesis is that all that was said above about what is operative in the hermeneutical movement from biblical text to "sermon" is also true with respect to what happens in the transposition of biblical texts into liturgical expressions for a service of worship. The triune God seeks to be enfleshed in *both* sermon *and* service *simultaneously*.

Tradition has tended to view Word and Sacrament as taking place side-by-side sequentially, in a service of worship, and, as we shall see later, there is an inherent sequence in the liturgical structure *from* Word *to* Sacrament. Yet from the perspective of the concept of proclamation as God's conversation with the community, Word and Sacrament are superimposed on each other simultaneously. The sermon is sacrament, and the sacrament is sermon, and everything that happens before and after and in between sermon and sacrament is all part of one event in which the Word of God happens. The movement from lectionary to liturgy and the crafting of worship in the shape of Scripture involves employing the same set of hermeneutical principles as one uses in creating sermons in the shape of Scripture. Liturgics and homiletics are partner disciplines joined in the worship leaders' common task of putting it all together for worship. The tools to shape the worship experience and to enable the community to be engaged by the Word of God are taken in hand from a common hermeneutical tool box. In the next chapter we shall look at how these disciplines merge in the shaping of the event.

THREE

Shaping the Event

The question that my preacher neighbor raised over the backyard fence more than a quarter century ago echoes in a question Professor Rice posed years later: "Can we find a place and a way to preach," he asks, "that faithfully resonate the Word of God seeking embodiment in bread, wine, water, human speech, and a community's interaction? Can we find a way of preaching that helps make all these factors and experiences an inseparable whole?"[1]

Daniel Stevick, who for years has guided the course of liturgical renewal, writes at the beginning of his *Crafting of Liturgy:*

The parts [of a liturgical event] should contribute to a convincing, satisfying whole. But there is a great deal that can go wrong. Elements can compete with or subvert one another. The strength of the spoken texts can be weakened by hymns that are too subjective, if they are not mawkishly sentimental. Strong, colorful ingredients can follow one another so closely that none of them shows up to advantage. Runaway virtuosity can heighten some nonessential action, while important acts are allowed to pass unnoticed. Or the liturgical event can be experienced as a series of parts that follow one another without shape, consecutiveness, or flow. If the parts of an act of worship are to contribute to one another and if together they are to fashion a whole, there is need for care, for criteria, for thought, discrimination, and priorities. Shaping good liturgy is a craft. Rather than being a science, it is an art, calling for taste, judgement, and design.[2]

32

As one who approaches liturgy from an Anglican perspective, Stevick recognizes that *The Book of Common Prayer* is the given framework for his recommendations. "Preparing worship," he continues, "in a church with an authorized liturgical text and preparing in a church without such a text are markedly different tasks. To adapt something that Robert Frost said about poetic meter and free verse: One is like playing tennis with a net and a marked court; the other is like playing tennis on an open field."[3]

What about those worship leaders serving on open fields? What approaches are appropriate and necessary for worship leaders in those settings that identify themselves with what is commonly called the "free-church" tradition? This chapter aims to show that Stevick's goal of liturgy to create a convincing, satisfying whole is possible also in those churches *without* authorized liturgical texts printed in prayer books or hymnals that are in the hands of each worshiper weekly. It is indeed, in Stevick's words, "a markedly different task" for leaders to prepare worship for congregations not accustomed to doing liturgy from an authorized text even though the denominational parent-bodies may have prepared such texts. Generally these liturgies prepared by denominational commissions and sometimes authorized by wider-church bodies appear in separate handbooks that are designed primarily for use by pastors and worship leaders. Some services also may be bound within hymnals for congregational use. Nevertheless, the worship leader has the awesome responsibility of choosing or creating worship expressions in the weekly task of crafting a community's corporate liturgy.

My pastor neighbor who was playing on an open field had a much more difficult task in "putting it all together" than another pastor living down the street whose task was primarily to choose hymns and to prepare a sermon "to go along with" the scripture readings. Crafting worship in which there are variables from week to week and choices of settings and even expectations of the leader to author original prayers and other worship expressions demands a significant commitment of time, energy, and expertise. My focus is to provide some assistance to those who feel they are playing on an open field and to share some markers and suggestions to help delineate the process so that worship leaders need not feel they are lobbing liturgical tennis balls aimlessly.

Organic Liturgy

Unfortunately, sometimes the free-church tradition has interpreted its freedom from adherence to prescribed liturgical texts as a license for an anything-goes approach to worship. Yet the goal of a liturgy that aims at a unified event is not to create a monolithic service revolving around some central theme. Thematic services based on holiday celebrations or on topics that are of the worship leader's preference often are manipulative and designed to have the worshipers experience what the leader wants them to experience. I choose, rather, to designate a liturgy in which all parts work together as an *organic* liturgy. All the individual acts, like the sermon, *grow out* of an engagement with the biblical texts and interact with each other homiletically and liturgically to enable the *leitourgia,* literally the "work," of the worshiping congregation to take place.

Liturgy is the totality of what happens verbally and nonverbally when the people of God find themselves in dialogue with the triune God who initiates the conversation and seeks to become enfleshed in the event of Word and Sacrament. The interconnectedness associated with an organic approach to liturgy is fundamentally a reflection of the very nature of the church itself, in New Testament images, as the *body* of Christ with Christ at the center and all the members working in harmony. The whole of worship is a total event of integrally related and mutually dependent acts through which the Word of God seeks embodiment in the community of faith.

A helpful way to visualize organic interconnectedness is through an artistic technique called pointillism, which was developed by French Post-Impressionist artists in the nineteenth century. In pointillism the total artistic creation, sometimes even including a "frame" around the scene, is the result of a mosaic of individual dots of pure color. These artists' experiments with the palette and brush foreshadowed by a hundred years what now through electronic means is created through a matrix of dots on a video monitor. Viewed up close what is seen on the artist's canvas and the video monitor is a collage of dots of individual unblended colors. At a distance, however, the dots together form a blended and unified image in the viewer's mind.

The role of the worship leader is to allow the Scriptures to shape a series of individual expressions that, in their totality, will enable the worship community to experience a unified event. The form and content of the painting will vary with the form and content of the biblical text. According to Professor Paul Wilson, "We could trace the seeds of this [approach] to William Wordsworth and Samuel Taylor Coleridge who helped revolutionize our approach to art. It was their idea that art has organic unity — all the parts work together to form a unified meaning."[4]

The quest for organic liturgy has been around for a long time. In worship traditions that follow authorized liturgies printed in prayer books or hymnals it has been the practice of clergy and church musicians to coordinate the musical expressions of the day with the spoken parts of the liturgy. In the free-church tradition leaders attempt to pick hymns that reinforce the theme of the sermon. But the purpose here is to explore in a more radical way how biblical texts can be interpreted in all liturgical acts so that these liturgical acts will *grow out* of the texts themselves and be shaped by the texts into an organic whole. It is the inherent unity between the text and the retextualization of that text into a variety of worship expressions that will create an organic unity among all the parts of the worship service. We shall address the process of creating individual liturgical expressions in the shape of Scripture in the next chapter. But first we need to address the shaping of the event itself.

The Structure of the Event

The concept of the worship event as an organic whole is related to an inherent *structure* of the sequence of interrelated communal actions that happen in the Word-event when the community is in conversation with the Word. It is this "sequence of parts coherently fulfilling one complete action" that Gregory Dix sixty years ago identified as "the shape of the liturgy."[5] Ever since that work, which has become both a monument and a marker in the liturgical renewal movement, liturgiologists have spoken of the "shape" or "shaping" of liturgy. Early studies like Dix's tended to speak of "the" liturgy as though there was an immutable and unalterable set of words and actions that had a definite and identifiable "shape."

Lately, particularly in the aftermath of the liturgical revolution of the 1960s and 1970s, it is difficult to attach a definitive "the" to liturgy with the singularness, maybe even the exclusivity, with which these earlier scholars viewed the subject. Given the multiplicity of options and alternatives in worship books, as evidenced in the 2006 *Evangelical Lutheran Worship,*[6] in which there are ten alternate settings of the Holy Communion, liturgiologists have tended to speak in the more dynamic verb-form language of "shaping." Even in the Roman Catholic missal with its once immutable singular set of words of the canon ("canon" literally means "fixed"), a number of variations have been provided. "Canon" has been re-interpreted to mean that what is "fixed" is the *structure,* but the priest is given the freedom to choose one of the optional settings of the eucharistic prayer suitable to the theme of the day. One Roman Catholic apologist writes, "In a sense, this variety and flexibility reflects the origins and present text of the Roman canon — 'fixed' in the sense of containing the same structure but varying within itself."[7]

Moreover, the structured sequence of actions we call liturgy is not stored in the printed pages of prayer books in pew racks but is shaped in the corporate memory of the community and is reshaped as the community is in continuing dialogue with God and the world through Scripture. "To be continued" might be the epilogue printed each week at the end of the order of service in worship bulletins or fliers. The place of continuation of the dialogue is obviously the world-setting of that particular community, but also the conversation is to be continued the next time the community gathers again for worship. Liturgy assumes a continual community of memory in which what will happen next Sunday is written over without erasing whatever happened last Sunday. Next Sunday's encounter with the Word of God will be patterned after last Sunday's experience, yet there will be nuances of reshaping as the community and the world in which the community lives and moves and has its being is shaped again by the God who makes all things new.

What is the source of this shaping? What pattern has patterned the peculiar sequence of events we call liturgy? Frank Senn, in his opus on liturgy that was twenty years in the making, concludes, "Much liturgical commentary in the twentieth century has been based on the premise that there is a pattern in liturgical worship that goes back to early descriptions of the liturgy, such as that in Justin Martyr's *Apology*. This basic shape comprises what has come to be seen as a four-movement structure of gathering, the word, the meal, and the dismissal."[8] He adds:

> Even among the Puritans who eschewed *The Book of Common Prayer,* this ecumenical order was followed. John Cotton's *The True Constitution of a Particular Visible Church Proved by Scripture* (London, 1642)

provided an order of worship that included the following: opening prayers of thanksgiving and intercession, the singing of psalms, reading and expounding the Word of God in sermons, exhortation to the congregation, questioning of the preacher by the laity, and celebrating the Lord's Supper "once a month at least."[9]

Liturgiologists in a variety of communities who have researched the history of liturgical development all point to this basic structure that has evolved in the worship life of the Christian community over the centuries and that shares a common shape regardless of the uniquenesses of particular denominations and local church practices. This common shape is called the "ordo," the basic pattern of "one thing set next to another"[10] in an ordered sequence. Hence, "Order of Worship" often becomes the heading at the beginning of the worship section of church bulletins.

Senn includes a comparison chart of the Post–Vatican II "Order of Mass" in the *Roman Missal* (1969), the order for "Holy Communion" in the *Lutheran Book of Worship* (1979), the order for "The Holy Eucharist" in the Episcopal *Book of Common Prayer* (1977), the "Service of Word and Table" in *The United Methodist Hymnal* (1989), and the "Service for the Lord's Day" in *Book of Common Worship* (1993) of the Presbyterian Church USA.[11] He notes, "The common shape of liturgy in these five traditions is more remarkable than the differences."[12] At least three more orders in the Reformed tradition could be added to Senn's list: "The Service of Word and Sacrament" in the *Psalter Hymnal* of the Christian Reformed Church (1987), the "Order of Worship" of the Reformed Church in America included in *Rejoice in the Lord* (1985), and "Service of Word and Sacrament I and II" in *Book of Worship* of the United Church of Christ (1986). The two UCC liturgies are inclusive-language revisions of orders first published in 1966 and 1969 respectively. Since Senn created his chart, the Evangelical Lutheran Church in America published *Evangelical Lutheran Worship*.

Further, the list could be expanded ecumenically to include the liturgies created by the Consultation on Church Union, through the *Baptism, Eucharist and Ministry* conversations, and by the ecumenical committee that created a liturgy to celebrate the *Formula of Agreement* between the Evangelical Lutheran Church in America, the Presbyterian Church USA, the Reformed Church in America, and the United Church of Christ. These additions serve to reinforce Senn's observation that the common shape of the liturgy reflected in each of these denominational traditions is truly remarkable.

As we review the dates when these were published, we can begin to grasp the extraordinary liturgical work accomplished over a forty-year period by individual denominational agencies and also by ecumenical bodies. The common understanding of the shape of Christian worship that has emerged from the liturgical renewal movement now makes possible an ecumenical approach to the teaching of worship in theological seminaries and lay academies. Although worship has ecclesiastical and cultural uniquenesses indigenous to each community, it is less denominationally specific than was once imagined. The shape of liturgy is in the common domain of the ecumenical faith community and cannot be assigned a legal copyright or denominational imprimatur.

The liturgical movement of the second half of the twentieth century rested on new understandings of the nature of history that developed a century earlier. The prejudices that became entrenched following the Reformation of the sixteenth century colored how the church traced its history. To many in the Protestant camp there was a great hiatus in God's story that stopped with the closure of the New Testament canon, perhaps stretched a bit to include the ante-Nicean church, and then somehow miraculously revived itself in the sixteenth century. A millennium of the church's being and doing somehow was overlooked.

As a result of the work of Continental Idealist philosophers and theologians, church historians in England and America learned a new historiography that enabled them to trace church history not around but through the medieval Roman Catholic Church. Such understandings fueled the Anglo-catholic movement in the Anglican communions and energized the Mercersburg movement in the German Reformed Church in the United States. Scholars began to see the church's worship life in continuity with what tradition had continued to shape during that perceived thousand-year pause in God's conversation. Ones who feared to tread on well-entrenched prejudices could now trace their own Protestant worship traditions through catholic eyes, in the universal sense of the word "catholic."

Yet it has taken, at least here in America, nearly a century of theological and liturgical distractions for the work of nineteenth-century scholars to be realized in the liturgical shapings that now are common in the ecumenical community. As the liturgies of the 1970s and 1980s were being produced by the various churches, I assigned my students to trace their own denominational liturgies back through their historic antecedents to the liturgies of the Reformation and their roots in the medieval Roman Catholic Church. One book of primary sources was Bard Thompson's *Liturgies of the Western Church,* a collection of representative liturgies ranging from the First Apology of Justin Martyr to John Wesley's Sunday Service.[13] Students learned that although there were some deviations due to other forces in the church's life over time, there was a common shape that ran throughout the history of their own denominations' liturgical practices. Moreover, as they traced their own denominational heritages, they discovered that their colleagues of traditions other than their own were finding the same common thread.

Much of the liturgical discussions in the sixteenth and seventeenth centuries in Europe — or the ecclesiastical divisions that ensued for lack of consensus — centered around how much or how little of the Roman Catholic mass was to be retained in the churches of the Reformation. There were those, like Luther, who felt that as long as the liturgical expressions did not contradict their interpretations of Scripture, the traditional wordings and orders of the mass could remain *adiaphora,* indifferences. There were those, like the English Puritans, who adopted the opposite opinion, namely, that the Scriptures themselves should dictate the form and content of worship.

The Middleburg Liturgy of the English Puritans (1586), for example, sought, as indicated in its subtitle, to be "agreeable to Gods worde and the vse of the reformed Churches."[14] Scripture was authoritative not only in doctrine but in all of the Christian life including worship practices, and the Middleburg Liturgy sought to bring about worship reform by insuring that each liturgical expression had to have its warrant in Scripture. Guided more by doctrinal considerations than by hermeneutical principles, Reformation and post-Reformation worship renewal in general was premised on warranting inherited liturgical words and actions by trying to find some "agreement" for these in the texts of Scripture.

After the Restoration of the monarchy in England in 1660, Charles II issued the *Declaration concerning Ecclesiastical Affairs,* in which he promised to appoint "an equal number of learned divines of both persuasions" to review and revise the Prayer Book and to provide alternative forms in scriptural wordings so that the minister might use "one or the other at his discretion."[15] Political expediency may have been the king's motive, but it is truly remarkable that the idea of including alternative liturgical expressions to the Prayer Book was proposed as early as 1660. Moreover the assumption that such variant wordings would accomplish the same liturgical intention sounds like what was being proposed by the reformers of worship practice in the 1960s.

The convocation took place in the spring of 1661 in Savoy. The "learned divines" could not agree, but in the heat of the squabble, one of their number, Richard Baxter, "in a fortnight" produced a complete liturgy constructed of biblical speech, known as "The Savoy Liturgy" of 1661. Baxter's intention was to demonstrate that a complete liturgy could be drawn from the Scriptures and constructed in biblical language. "It was," Thompson said, "a realization of the Puritan desire to have an exact correspondence between worship and the Word of God. Baxter was persuaded that such a liturgy would comprehend all manner of Christians . . . ; and all would be free to interpret this liturgy 'according to the sense they have in Scripture.'"[16]

Liturgy Shaped by Scripture

Since ancient times Christian liturgies have included language and images lifted directly from the Scriptures. The Sanctus ("Holy, holy, holy"), based on Isaiah 6:3 and Revelation 4:8, is believed to have become part of the eucharistic liturgy in Alexandria somewhere around 230 C.E. The Gloria in Excelsis, the song of the angels at Jesus' birth according to Luke 2:14, was introduced in the Western rite in the middle of the fourth century. The Hebrew Bible's 150 psalms recited or chanted were a liturgical part of Christian worship from the beginning of the church's life.

A reading of the New Testament, particularly in the New Revised Standard Version, reveals that many of the indented passages, some of which are transpositions of texts from the Old Testament, were liturgical materials that through the community's worship became part of the tradition that ultimately was canonized as Scripture. The book of Revelation particularly is studded with liturgical expressions that the writer included to assure the community in very tough times that God was in charge and would bring a new order into being. As early as the second century Justin Martyr proposed that worship should focus on what he called "the good things" or "beautiful things" of the Bible.[17] Clearly the liturgical use of scripture texts has been part of the Christian worship experience from the earliest days of the church's life.

What has rarely been admitted by liturgical scholars until quite recently is that the *form* or *shape* of the worship event itself arises from the Scriptures. Sixty years ago Gregory Dix categorically stated that the shape of eucharistic worship from the outset "was not based on scripture at all, whether of the Old or New Testament, but solely on *tradition*."[18] However, Gordon Lathrop two generations later begins his liturgical theology with a very significant chapter titled "The Biblical Pattern of Liturgy." He says:

> Start with the Bible.... The Bible marks and largely determines Christian corporate worship.... Ancient texts are used to speak a new grace.... The liturgical pattern is drawn from the Bible.... The scheduling of the *ordo,* the setting of one liturgical thing next to another in the shape of the liturgy, evokes and replicates the deep structure of biblical language.[19]

Contemporary Reformed theologian E. H. Van Olst affirms as the central thesis of his book *The Bible and Liturgy* "that the structure of celebration is a given that comes with Scripture itself. In terms of both origin and use the Bible can be called a liturgical book."[20] It is interesting to see the shift that is occurring in liturgical scholarship regarding the role of Scripture in the shaping of liturgy.

Four hundred years ago the Puritans were concerned about the *content* of liturgy and its scriptural warrant, and they went *back* to the Bible texts in their search to purify the church's worship. Today some of us are concerned also about the *shaping* of the worship experience and with the aid of a newer hermeneutic allowing the Scriptures to encounter us *in front of* the text to structure our liturgical conversation with the Word of God each time the Christian community gathers for corporate worship. The shaping of the worship event, therefore, is not something imposed from the outside but *is inherent in the nature of the event itself.* The structure of the liturgical experience, like the content, also is organic, growing out of the very shape of the Scriptures themselves. I propose that we can discover the structure of the Word-event in the biblical texts themselves, and the shape that emerges will be similar to the common shape of the liturgy that emerges by comparing contemporary denominational liturgies and by tracing their historical antecedents.

The Bible is a record of the conversations between God and the people of God, and there is a particular structure or shape integral to each conversation. Scholars working on literary genres and particularly narrative forms in the Bible have pointed out the inherently dynamic nature of the texts. There is an intrinsic movement in the texts: "a" leads to "b," and "b" leads to "c," and so forth. Concerning "shaping sermons by the structure of the text," William Carl III writes: "Listening to Scripture and its different forms is like listening to music and learning to hear with a trained ear. It is like learning to hear the theme of a Bach fugue as it makes its way from part to part."[21]

Furthermore, since worship is primarily an oral event, the mode of the divine-human conversation is dialogical. God speaks; the community responds. The community asks; God answers. Worship is God's conversation with the people of God and the community's communication with the divine Communicator. Hence, the shape the worship conversation takes will be dialogical. The psalms, some of the most ancient liturgical acts that the community has preserved, reveal an inherent dialogical form. The heading "*Responsive* Readings" (emphasis added) in many older hymnals gives us a hint of the form not only of the psalms but of all homiletical and liturgical acts. Generally the dialogues are printed in bulletins or worship books or projected on screens so that the various participants may speak the words assigned them.

However, in some ethnic communities, particularly in African American worship, spontaneous dialogue frequently takes place between the worship leader and the congregation as part of the liturgical action, most often in the sermon. Participatory preaching as practiced in these communities is a homiletical and liturgical patterning that is far more faithful to the biblical mode of God's self-disclosure than the three-points-and-a-poem sermon-structure inherited from Enlightenment rationalism. "Dialogue sermons" were popularized during the liturgical revolutions of the 1960s and 1970s. They tended to be topical, sometimes in the form of a debate between proponents of opposite positions. There is a way of shaping sermons, particularly on long scripture passages, that becomes a dialogue between one person who reads a certain portion of the text and another person who preaches on that portion of the text; the dialogical pattern continues, in turn, through the other portions of the lectionary text. I have found this form particularly helpful in preaching on lengthy passages such as the healing of the man born blind (John 1:1–41) and the raising of Lazarus (John 11:1–44).

If one can shape a sermon by the structure of a biblical text, cannot also a liturgy be shaped by the structure of the same biblical text so that, like a fugue, the biblical theme will be heard in many variations and voices throughout the worship event? The classic text for the shaping of a liturgy is Isaiah 6:1–9a (Isaiah's temple experience), but the same shape emerges in what happens in Moses' encounter with the burning bush (Exod. 3:1–4:17), in the annunciation to Mary (Luke 1:26–38), and in Jesus' feeding of the five thousand (Matt. 14:13–23, Mark 6:30–46, Luke 9:10–17, John 6:1–15),[22] just to mention a few.

Did not the fourfold shape of the liturgy that emerged quite early in the life of the Christian community have the same shape as many biblical texts that the community experienced in its encounter with the Word of God? And could it not be that the strikingly common shape of the community's conversation even in different denominational settings today is due not only to what centuries of repetition began to store in the community's memory but also by the community's continual encounter, even unconsciously, with the biblical texts and their own inherent shapings of what happens in the Word event today? The early observance of Palm Sunday, for example, grew out of the life of the Jerusalem church as in liturgical pilgrimage it reenacted, step by step, the scriptural story of Jesus' entry into Jerusalem and experienced again through the liturgical action the meaning of the Word recontextualized: "Blessed is the One who comes in the name of the Lord." The pattern of the worship experience itself was shaped by the Scripture text.

On the other hand, there are scripture texts that have been shaped by liturgical use prior to their being included in literary forms in the Bible. The beloved hymn to love in 1 Corinthians 13 is believed by some scholars to have emerged in the liturgical life of the early Christian community and was inserted into the letter to the Corinthian church as an illustration of the "still more excellent way" of relating to one another of which Paul was speaking at the end of chapter 12. There are many other worship expressions in both Testaments that had their origins outside the biblical texts and found their way into the Scripture because they were part of the shared liturgical memory of the worshiping communities in which biblical texts were shaped. We can say, then, that there are instances in which worship shaped Scripture just as Scripture shapes worship today.

Obviously there are those texts in which there is no theophany as in the illustrative narrative texts mentioned above. The genealogies in the book of Numbers, for example, hardly evoke a sense of homiletical and liturgical structure. Yet interestingly, the writers of both the Gospels of Matthew and Luke include genealogies as parts of their birth narratives. So these texts need to be seen in light of the larger narrative of God's self-disclosure and the overall structure of the theophany to which the Scriptures testify. One of the sermons I remember from years past was an Advent sermon based on the genealogy in Matthew's birth narrative. What made it memorable was not any references to the text itself but the way in which the preacher allowed the genealogy to be interpreted as part of a total Advent worship experience of Christ's coming that was shaped by the larger narrative of Matthew's Gospel in which the genealogy was embedded.

Simply to restrict liturgy, and preaching, to narrative genres would be terribly exclusive and rob congregations of the richness of the Scriptures. But where, then, is the inherent structure that shapes these individual expressions into an organic whole? We need to see individual texts within the context of the wider structure of the divine-human interaction to which the whole Bible testifies. Hence, the liturgical structure that enables the individual expressions arising out of non-narrative biblical genres, such as letters, laws, songs, poetry, sayings, to be shaped into an organic liturgy will be informed by the overall pattern of the divine self-disclosure that arises out of Scripture as a whole.

There are times when the common liturgical structure that emerges from Bible and tradition can shape non-narrative texts into organic liturgies. There are times, too, when an individual text needs to be interpreted homiletically and liturgically within the context of other texts. The *Revised Common Lectionary* provides multiple texts for each Sunday and special holy days in the church year. Sometimes the structure of the worship event arises out of the movement from one text to another text, and the overall experience is shaped by the larger scriptural metanarrative of which the individual texts are part. We shall see some examples of the way multiple texts shape a worship service in the next chapter.

At other times, with the mere juxtaposition of one lection with another the worship event becomes structured according to the overall biblical and historic pattern. This may mean, for example, that a Gospel lesson such as the narrative of the feeding of the five thousand may come *after* the sermon as a preface to the eucharist and thereby create a dynamic link between Word and Sacrament. Such decisions are part of the process of orchestrating liturgy that I will discuss in greater detail in chapter 5.

The Shape of Divine-Human Interaction

Ultimately at the heart of the shaping of the sequence of events that make up a worship service is the inner dynamic of the divine-human interaction to which the Scriptures as a whole testify and that is reflected in the texts themselves. Let us analyze the structure, as textualized in Scripture, of the three encounters cited above, namely, Moses' encounter with God on Sinai, the annunciation to Mary, and Jesus' feeding of the five thousand.

Each interaction begins at God's initiative or at least with a human perception that something beyond human enterprise is about to happen:

"There [on Horeb, the mountain of God] the angel of the Lord appeared to [Moses] in a flame of fire out of a bush." (Exod. 3:2)

"[The angel] came to [Mary] and said, 'Greetings, favored one! The Lord is with you.'" (Luke 1:28)

"[Jesus] said to them, 'Come away to a deserted place all by yourselves and rest a while.'" (Mark 6:31)

The texts point to some divine interruption of human everydayness with a Word, sometimes accompanied by some other theophany, calling the individuals and the community to an awareness of a holy otherness of presence and a sacredness of place to which the encounter gathers them. The divine intruders announce that something extra-ordinary is about to happen that may transform ordinary places such as a pasture into holy ground and a barren desert into the green grass that becomes the setting for a eucharistic feast.

Second, there is some human awareness and acknowledgment of a discontinuity between the divine and the human, sometimes even a questioning of the extraordinariness, even a repeated interrogation of the divine intruder:

Then Moses said, "I must turn aside and look at this great sight. . . . "
Then [Yahweh] said, "Come no closer! Remove the sandals from your
feet, for the place on which you are standing is holy ground. . . . " And
Moses hid his face, for he was afraid to look at God. (Exod. 3:3, 5, 6b)

But [Mary] was much perplexed by [the angel's] words and pondered
what sort of greeting this might be. (Luke 1:29)

[The disciples] said to him, "Are we to go and buy two hundred
denarii worth of bread, and give it to them to eat?" (Mark 6:37b)

In each text the human reaction to the divine interruption is a "But how
can this be?" The disjuncture causes an awareness of one's humanness,
as in Isaiah's temple experience (see the table on page 57). "Woe is me!
I am lost, for I am a man of unclean lips and I live among a people of
unclean lips." Noteworthy is the continuation of the sentence, regardless
of which conjunction, "for" or "yet," is inserted: "Yet my eyes have seen
the King, the Lord of hosts!" (Isa. 6:5). In the presence of the divine,
humans are made aware of their humanness, and the perception of the
disjuncture prompts what sometimes is called confession. However, since
"confession" is still a hot-button liturgical issue in some quarters, I prefer
the more generic "penitence," from the Latin *paenitentia,* "repentance."
In the presence of the divine interruption, there is a pause for human
reflection, for questioning one's own humanness, for turning toward the
divine alternative, and for asking for a forgiveness that comes from beyond
human imagination.

The human questioning is followed by a Word, a divine Word, spoken
to assure the human that at-one-ness with the divine is promised and that
a Word of judgment and grace is forthcoming from the divine side. God
has something to say to the people of God:

"I have observed the misery of my people who are in Egypt . . . and
I have come down to deliver them. . . . So come, I will send you to
Pharaoh to bring my people . . . out of Egypt. . . . I will be with you."
(Exod. 3:7–8a, 10, 12a)

The angel said to her, "Do not be afraid, Mary, for you have found
favor with God." (Luke 1:30)

[Jesus] said to them, "How many loaves have you? Go and see." When they had found out, they said, "Five, and two fish." Then he ordered them to get all the people to sit down in groups on the green grass. (Mark 6:38–39)

Notice in the last passage that what was formerly a deserted place, literally, a desert-place, *eremos* in Greek, now suddenly is a pasture green with grass. When a bush burns and a virgin is pregnant and a desert greens, holy things are about to happen! The Word spoken will become the Word enacted.

In both Moses' encounter on Sinai and Mary's visitation by an angel, there is no feeding sequence as in the last story. Yet, despite Moses' repeated protests and questionings of his fitness for God's mission of deliverance, there is an implicit response; he will respond and go and do what God is commanding. Mary, following a second questioning of how she could bear a son while yet a virgin, nevertheless offered herself: "Here am I, the servant of the Lord; let it be with me according to your word." In most contemporary liturgies, when the eucharist is not celebrated the offering is a foreshadowing of a later eucharistic meal. And when the eucharist is celebrated, the offering is also a time for preparing the table with the bread and wine.

In the story of the feeding of the five thousand, the action continues after the five loaves and two fish have been found:

Taking the five loaves and the two fish, [Jesus] looked up to heaven, and blessed and broke the loaves, and gave them to his disciples to set before the people. . . . And all ate and were filled. (Mark 6:41–42)

The divine-human interaction is completed in the eating. Gregory Dix identified the four verbs "take," "bless," "break," and "give," in this passage and in the other texts recounting the institution in the upper room meal, as the "four-action shape of the Eucharist."[23] In a footnote Gordon Lathrop takes exception to Dix's identification of four separate actions, saying that the four are a single, unified action of thanksgiving or eucharist.[24] Nevertheless, what Dix identified was a sequence of actions, obviously all part of one event, that were derived from the earliest communities' celebration and that became part of the New Testament witness in the synoptic narration of the Last Supper (Matt. 26:26–29, Mark 14:22–25, Luke 22:17–20) and in the Pauline repetition in 1 Corinthians 11:23–26.

For us today, in structuring liturgy in the shape of Scripture Dix's identification of the four-action sequence is quite helpful, and equally instructive is Lathrop's note that the whole meal is a unified act of thanksgiving.

Finally, the divine-human interaction concludes with some form of dismissal or sending:

> [To Moses] God said, "Now go, and I will be with your mouth and teach you what you are to speak." (Exod. 4:12)

> Then the angel departed from her [and] . . . Mary set out and went with haste to a Judean town in the hill country, where she entered the house of Zechariah and greeted Elizabeth. (Luke 1:38b–40)

> Immediately [Jesus] made his disciples get into the boat and go on ahead . . . while he dismissed the crowd. (Mark 6:45)

The structure of each interaction leads to another encounter. Each text ends with an implicit "to be continued." In the drama of the divine-human interaction there is yet another act to follow, and there are specific action-words in the texts that indicate that the present chapter in the divine-human interaction is complete and that send the human participants onward to the next encounter. There is always a commissioning for doing the unfinished work that has begun in the worship event itself, work that will take place in many settings where the people of God live out their baptismal vocation. And amid the sending there is always a blessing and assurance that God will be with them in the accomplishment of the work. There is always an immediacy about getting on with the work. God seems not to like folks to linger long, for God has something else in mind for them to do.

Divine-Human Interaction in Worship

As each of these examples illustrates, texts of Scripture themselves have an inherent structure that is patterned after the very nature of God's ways of engaging in conversation with the people of God. This intrinsic pattern is what is at the heart of all liturgy, and the pattern is fivefold: (1) Gathering, (2) Penitence, (3) Word, (4) Offertory/Eucharist, and (5) Sending or Dismissal. The table on page 57 shows the basic structure of a service of Word and Sacrament juxtaposed with the actions intrinsic to Isaiah

6:1–9. Even though there is no direct linkage to the eucharist in this Old Testament text, nevertheless, as in Christian worship services in which the eucharist is not celebrated, the offertory element prefigures what happens in the offering of elements that prefaces the celebration of the eucharist.

Some liturgiologists include the Penitential act under the Gathering heading. I maintain that it is helpful to identify the Penitential part distinctly because, in the first place, confession traditionally was a rite separate from the mass itself, and, secondly, there is still a lingering, maybe even growing, aversion to the need for corporate acknowledgment of sin in both church and the secular culture. There is a need to ask for and receive forgiveness that is essential to individual and societal wholeness.

It is this common pattern that is reflected in the remarkably similar shape of the denominational liturgies and their historic antecedents. And it is this pattern that can allow texts to recontextualize themselves in the shaping of the community's liturgy. So the old argument of liturgical worship versus nonliturgical worship is really moot. All worship that seeks to engage Scripture and allows the Word of Scripture to become recontextualized organically in the life of a worshiping community will be inherently liturgical because the Bible itself is a liturgical book.

Although there have been listings of the parts or separate actions of the liturgy since the days of Justin Martyr, headings such as I enumerated above are arbitrary and serve more an educational function than a liturgical one. The parts, although individually identifiable, are sequences in *a continuum of actions* that together shape the worship event. The *Book of Common Worship* of the Presbyterian Church USA includes a very helpful description of the order for Word and Sacrament that I have used frequently in workshops for pastors and lay leaders.[25] The subtitle to the "Service for the Lord's Day" is noteworthy: "A Description of Its *Movement* and *Elements* [emphasis added]." These are dynamic words reflecting the inner movement from one element to another in the liturgical action. There is an intrinsic rhythm that moves the worship service through a continuum of elements, some of which are joyous and celebrative, others introspective and contemplative. Sometimes there are even moments of sheer silence. Yet unless it is a silence of interruption caused by leadership snafus, that silence is part of the inner dynamic of the divine-human encounter.

Such movement is not some external shape imposed on the worship event. Rather the action grows out of the very movement intrinsic to the biblical texts themselves as they reflect the shaping that the Word of God is effecting in the worship event. God *moves* in a mysterious way in the encounter with the people of God, and they discover that at the conclusion of the worship event they are at a different place spiritually than they were when they were first called into the encounter. Something happens when God acts. People are moved — in multileveled meanings of that word — and are shaped into new beings in the image of God.

Liturgy, therefore, is neither a tradition-dictated canon of authorized worship words printed in a gilt-edged book nor a random collection of worship expressions photocopied into a worship folder. Liturgy is a unified order of sequenced actions that has a shape made possible by an undergirding structure arising from the very form of the Word-event itself. The enduring legacy of Frank Lloyd Wright in his search for what he called "organic architecture," in which the building, its furnishings, and its setting are organically related to each other, is the dictum that "form follows function." In liturgy also, form follows function. The *form* or shape liturgy takes follows the *function* of the Word-event which is witnessed to in the biblical texts and practiced in the ongoing conversation and liturgical action of the community. In the end, the function of the Word-event is the proclamation of the one Word, Jesus Christ, seeking embodiment in the life of Christ's body. To that end the homiletical and liturgical tasks are wedded. They are in partnership to plan, to craft, and to lead everything the community does in this ordered sequence of interrelated actions so that, at least from the human side, this corporate conversation may be open to becoming an event of the Word of God.

Individual worshipers in a congregation come to the communal event with differing preunderstandings and predispositions that will shape their own encounters with the Word in uniquely different and individualized molds. The life-texts the community brings to the worship place are not all from the same book, nor even from the same library. Each text is unique to each individual, especially in an age of diversity and in a society that has individualized and privatized the faith experience. Different people are engaged by some worship expressions more than by others, as the studies cited earlier indicate. It took an astute director of music to teach me that, since people are not engaged equally in the worship event, liturgy needs to provide a variety of expressions on the same biblical theme or text in order to bring about a sense of corporateness in the worship experience.

The community will allow the *texts* of the expressions in the ordered sequence of the liturgy to be changed from Sunday to Sunday. Texts of hymns and sermons, like the scripture texts prescribed in the lectionary, change weekly in even the most prescribed of prayer-book traditions. But to change the *order* in which these expressions occur could result in a liturgical rebellion in even the freest of free-church traditions! Although individual worshipers have favorite hymns and congregations have beloved responses, what is stored in the congregation's *corporate* memory is the structured sequence, the shape, the order of the service. One pastor, I am told, decided on the Sunday after Easter to reverse the order of the liturgy, and so the service began with the benediction and worked backwards to the call to worship! When asked by one irate parishioner what the rationale was for this backwards liturgy, the pastor reportedly replied, "I just wanted to shake them up." Worship can be a shaking-up event when God does the shaking, but worship leaders do not have license to abort for novelty's sake a structure that is intrinsic to Scripture itself and has been imprinted on the church's individual and corporate memory for nearly two thousand years.

In my days as a teacher of confirmands I regularly asked them to tell me verbally the order of what comes after what in that church's Sunday worship services. Those who were not newcomers to the church's worship could retrieve from memory the order of worship without a bulletin in hand, sometimes even reciting those expressions that through repetition had been stored in the church's corporate memory. As a parish pastor for twenty-seven years I was told on numerous occasions by persons from denominational traditions other than my own, particularly by Roman Catholics, "Pastor, the service is the same." Obviously there were some very great differences in ceremonial, style, and even liturgical texts, yet the sameness that those people perceived is the common structure that is at the heart of all Christian liturgy. It is not the wording that people remember and compare but the structure of what follows what that is stored in their individual and communal memory. It is this structure that provides continuity to each's community's worship life from Sunday to Sunday.

This discussion of structure has focused on the service of Word and Sacrament for the Lord's Day or, simply, what is considered the general Sunday worship experience. However, it is my contention that the same structure is inherent in occasional services as well, particularly in orders for marriage and burial. These services also are patterned after the same inherent structure in the divine-human interaction I outlined above.

The operative understanding of baptism/initiation is that this sacrament, like Holy Communion, or eucharist, is not a separate service but a sign-act integral to the Service of Word and Sacrament itself. It would be a source of joy if the bath of initiation were part of each Sunday's gathering. Yet even when there is no one to be baptized/initiated into a congregation's life, there are opportunities for rites of remembrance of baptism. The Apostles' Creed in dialogical form ("Do you believe in God?" "I believe in God, the Father Almighty . . . ") or even spoken in unison can be prefaced with the leader's invitation: "Let us profess the faith into which we are baptized. . . ." When I included the dialogical form of the Apostles' Creed, prefaced by the invitation to profess the faith into which we are baptized, one pastor whom tradition had conditioned to be "against creeds" said, "In that form the Apostles' Creed became a new way for me to affirm my faith." The Trinitarian baptismal formula, "In the name of the Father and of the Son and of the Holy Spirit," is a reminder that the gathering of the community is always predicated on the common baptism that constitutes the church. And the sending at the end of the worship event is a commissioning of the community to live out their baptismal vocation in world. The whole of the worship event finds its setting within the context of the baptismal bath that gathers and sends the community. It is fitting that both the gathering and sending take place at the font or pool — with water poured, sprinkled, dipped-into, and even applied onto the heads or foreheads of the assembly by the assembly! Worship is always an immersion, a plunge into the mystery of God. Therefore I believe fonts should never have lids and never remain dry!

If the service of Christian marriage is more than a legalization of a relationship and if the service of Christian burial is more than the extension of a wake, then these services will find a shaping very similar to the structure of the service of Word and Sacrament for the Lord's Day. Moreover, these occasional services also rightfully may include celebrations of the eucharist. The wedding culture has suggested the idea of communion to Protestants, probably as a carryover from the Roman Catholic nuptial mass, but somehow the eucharist was forgotten in Protestant ideas of burial rites, even before the days when these began to be conducted in funeral establishments. However, is it not very appropriate — that is, if all attending are invited to commune — to celebrate a one-ness in

Christ and at-one-ness with Christ through the eucharist in marriage and burial services? I have found in my pastoral ministry an increasing willingness to consider eucharist as part of these rites. Sometimes it simply takes appropriate suggestions and illustrations on the part of the worship leader.[26]

Within the common liturgical structure which all corporate worship experiences share are some individual components that I have been calling worship *expressions*. The *Book of Common Worship* describes them as "elements." These are the prayers, songs, readings, sermons, and other corporate acts — the individual dots — that occur in the structured sequence and that together constitute the liturgical action of a given worship experience. Studying the various liturgies created over time in vastly different worship communities one can see how expressions change from liturgy to liturgy and from week to week. These expressions are the individual ways in which biblical texts are enacted, and united together they form a common staging for the divine-human drama to take place. We shall explore what is involved in the shaping of these expressions in the next chapter.

Nevertheless, we need to pause to remember a single sentence stated over thirty years ago by one of the liturgical masters of the twentieth century. James White began his book *Christian Worship in Transition* with a chapter titled, "You are Free — If."[27] This treatise was written a decade after the worship revolution of the 1960s witnessed the great fall of all the liturgical humpty-dumpties that once provided security to worship leaders. White begins,

> During the decade ending in 1975, I had the opportunity to do workshops in some three dozen states for people responsible for planning and leading services of Christian worship. I always found, when all was said and done, that I had just one thing to say: "You are free — if. You are free — if you know what is essential in any type of worship."[28]

In almost half a century the worship revolution has taken many different courses and resulted in continuing battles among a variety of theological and liturgical camps. Yet the caution that Professor White sounded more than thirty years ago echoes with a certain contemporaneity germane to what we have been discussing in this chapter. You are free —

if you grasp the essential structure upon which the shaping of liturgy is premised.

Worship that is patterned after the fourfold or fivefold movement intrinsic to the nature of the divine-human interaction witnessed to in the Scriptures will provide a freedom for the community to enjoy — in the wonderful sense of the answer to the first question of the *Westminster Shorter Catechism* — new liturgical expressions. The structure also will ensure that the worshipers do not feel as though they are being bombarded by a series of liturgical tennis balls volleyed at them from an open field. The essential shape will bring worshipers closer to each other ecumenically, especially as such a variety of liturgical expressions arise out of the common texts from the *Common Lectionary*. The opposite, of course, leads to fragmentation in the Christian community and, as Marva Dawn reminds us, focuses on the worship leader's personality rather than on the God who is the Subject of worship.[29]

There also is need again for the reminder that the collection of individual expressions printed in a prayer book or in worship bulletins is not the liturgy. Liturgy, in the root meaning of *leitourgia*, is what occurs when the expressions are reenacted in what a congregation calls its worship "service." Liturgy, too, is that which gets embodied in its "work" of serving others outside the sacred sanctuary space. As such, *leitourgia* gets translated into *diakonia*. John Calvin did not include an offertory in the service he crafted for the community in Geneva, for he felt that the true offertory is what is expressed when the Christian meets the Christ in the neighbor. An organic liturgy not only will seek organicity among the various components of a particular worship service, it also will seek to be connected to that service which takes place when the worshipers leave the sanctuary. My mentor said more than thirty years ago:

> The English word "service" is a better translation of the Greek than "liturgy," for it has the same ambiguity of obedience and ministry on the one hand and of public worship on the other. As with Benedict's monks later, to work was to pray, or as Calvin has it, "lawful worship consists in obedience alone."[30]

The challenge that faces the worship leader as homiletician and liturgiologist is to craft both sermon and liturgy in such a way that different people will be enabled and equipped to enter into and to exit from the engagement with the texts at different places in the service and with differing degrees of involvement. Striving to allow the experience to emerge organically again is the key to this task. If the community is engaged in a conversation with a biblical text through a variety of genres in the liturgy, hopefully the individual engagements will add up to a corporate experience. Thus, as the surveys cited in the previous chapter indicated, one worshiper may be drawn into the conversation through the sermon, another through a corporate prayer, another through the singing of a hymn, another through an anthem, another through a story, another through a nonverbal or nonmusical act.

Furthermore, as educational models have proven, complementary expressions in a given worship event reinforce each other, and studies in oral communication show that repetition is the key to understanding in those acts of the worship experience that are primarily oral in nature. There is no opportunity for worshipers experiencing the Word orally to go back and reread something that happened previously in this sequence of actions. When the individual expressions in which the same text is transposed are enacted in the ordered sequence of a liturgical action, the worshiper can begin to detect, as in a piece of music, a common thread that runs throughout the service: "Ah, there it is again!" Sometimes one expression can be a harbinger of what will come later in the service. One pastor commented about what had preceded the sermon in a service of worship I crafted: "Throughout [earlier parts of] the liturgy, there was a faint echo of what was to come in the sermon."

An organic liturgy, therefore, is a unified action in which all the individual expressions in a worship service are recontextualized transpositions of the same biblical text(s) to enable these individualized points of engagement to be brought together into a corporate experience. All the expressions reinforce one another so that the whole is more than the sum of the parts. The goal of the liturgical art is worshipers' responding to the experience, as did one perceptive parishioner. Instead of the predictable "Good sermon, Pastor," he said to me on his way out of church, "Everything fit together today!"

Before we turn to the crafting of individual worship expressions, one final note to this chapter needs to be sounded. Liturgics and homiletics are servant arts, for worship ultimately is God's doing and acting. The words and actions of liturgy aim at allowing the Word of God to be heard and enfleshed in the community's encounter with God and one another.

The structure of the event is a human framework for God's shaping of the community in the image of God. The hermeneutical work of interpreting the texts of Scripture liturgically is to facilitate in finite human language the conversation that God intends to have with the community now. The French Impressionist painter Claude Monet said more than a hundred years ago that the purpose of art is, in a moment of time, to try to "capture the uncapturable." It can be said, likewise, that the role of homiletics and liturgics is to try to capture in the midst of a gathering of a unique assembly and in human words and actions what ultimately from the human perspective is uncapturable. Worship is a human event, in a given moment of human history, that nevertheless intends, in the words of Marva Dawn, to "immerse us in God's splendor."[31]

Basic Structure of a Service of Word and Sacrament
Paralleled with Isaiah's Temple Vision (Isa. 6:1–9)

GATHERING
  Call to worship
  Hymn or other act of praise

In the year that King Uzziah died, I saw the Lord sitting on a throne, high and lofty; and the hem of his robe filled the temple. Seraphs were in attendance above him; each had six wings: with two they covered their faces, and with two they covered their feet, and with two they flew. And one called to another and said: "Holy, holy, holy is the Lord of hosts; the whole earth is full of his glory." The pivots on the thresholds shook at the voices of those who called, and the house filled with smoke.

PENITENCE
  Call to repentance
  Prayer of confession
  Words of assurance
  Praise response

And I said: "Woe is me! I am lost, for I am a man of unclean lips, and I live among a people of unclean lips; yet my eyes have seen the King, the Lord of hosts!" Then one of the seraphs flew to me, holding a live coal that had been taken from the altar with a pair of tongs. The seraph touched my mouth with it and said: "Now that this has touched your lips, your guilt has departed and your sin is blotted out."

WORD
  Prayer for illumination
  Scripture lessons
  Sermon
  Affirmation of faith/
    Baptismal acts
  Prayers of the people

Then I heard the voice of the Lord saying, "Whom shall I send, and who will go for us?"

OFFERTORY/EUCHARIST
When eucharist is celebrated

When eucharist is not celebrated

And I said, "Here am I; send me!"

  Offertory, including
    presentation of elements
  Eucharistic prayer
  Breaking the bread and
    pouring the cup
  The Lord's Prayer
  Distribution
  Post-communion
    thanksgiving

  Offertory

  Prayer of thanksgiving

  The Lord's Prayer

SENDING
  Charge and/or Blessing
  Closing Hymn
  Departure

And [God] said, "Go..."

FOUR

Transposing the Texts

As I indicated in the previous chapter, the premise that lies behind the quest to create organic worship is that the same texts that are normative for the preparation of a sermon are also normative in the crafting of the liturgical expressions which will be part of the community's communal worship event. Hermeneutics, the art of interpretation, we also concluded earlier, is the unifying discipline that unites homiletics and liturgics in the communal conversation with the text. We turn, then, to explore how individual biblical texts prescribed by the *Revised Common Lectionary* can be crafted into liturgical expressions for a community's common conversation with the Word of God.

The Context for Recontextualization

The context in which texts are recontextualized is a Christian community, which brings to the conversations with the texts an unapologetically *Christian* set of presuppositions and preunderstandings. Other faith communities have developed their own hermeneutical perspectives, and it is not for us to judge the rightness or wrongness of their understandings. However, it is clear in the New Testament itself that the earliest communities employed a peculiar Christological hermeneutic in their interpretation of the Hebrew Scriptures as well as in their encounters with the other cultures in which the Gospel was proclaimed. And it is not inappropriate for the central profession that Jesus Christ is Lord to become the lens through which the church today does its witness and work, particularly its homiletical and liturgical tasks.

Louis Cranach the Elder was a sixteenth-century German artist who became a champion of the Lutheran reformation. One of his paintings is the center of the altarpiece in the Stadtkirche in Wittenberg, where Luther preached and did his liturgical and theological work. On the left side of the painting there is an assembly of solid-looking citizens, including Luther's wife, obviously looking very attentively toward the right side of the painting, where Luther is in the pulpit expounding the Word of God. With his left hand he is pointing to the scripture text in the open Bible. With his right hand he points to the center of the painting. What is so extraordinary is what appears in that middle section between the congregation on the left and Luther in the pulpit on the right: Christ on the cross. Luther was preaching, the congregation were listening, but what they saw was Christ crucified. To me that painting graphically portrays the homiletical and liturgical task before the church today: unapologetically in preaching and worship to speak and act in such ways that, although they are human words and actions, what is seen and heard is the One Word of God, Jesus Christ.

Each worshiper comes into the conversation with the texts with different needs and different expectations. Yet the Word that will be heard differently through different worship expressions in different hearts — I use intentionally here the biblical receptor — will involve, but will not be dependent on, what the hearers bring to the conversation. God in Christ is the Subject of worship, and the divine-human encounter begins with God. Each worshiper and the worshiping assembly as a community of faith bring to the encounter the baggage of their individual and communal life journeys. Yet the baggage itself, even though it may have been bounced around and bruised by less than humane handling, is not the primary subject of the conversation. People come expecting to hear what *God* will be saying and to encounter what *God* will be doing in the worship event. The journey toward the sacred by many in what Wade Clark Roof calls "a spiritual quest culture,"[1] despite the bulk of human baggage that gets dragged along, is a yearning somewhere somehow to be touched and handled by things unseen.

The religious yearning of a post-Enlightenment Western world in which transcendence, in the words of William Placher, has been "domesticated to fit our own human categories,"[2] is a search to rediscover a sense of the divine mystery that cannot be confined to what human reason has determined is reality. The experience that is the aim of worship is the experience *of*

God. God will speak and act as God will. If God is the rightful Subject of worship, then the worship leader cannot control what the community will experience. The worship expressions that the worship leader and the community create are simply earthen vessels, easily broken, easily discarded, easily forgotten, easily replaced, to steward but for an hour, maybe even a moment in God's time, the transcendent treasure that "belongs to God and does not come from us" (2 Cor. 4:7).

Interpreting texts liturgically is not a process of reducing the meaning of those texts to some universal rational principles or moral proverbs that will appeal in like manner to everyone's intellect. The community brings more than reason to the conversation. People bring their emotions, their quests for spirituality and mystery, their searches for sacramentality and wholeness, and the entire range of human experiences that lie within and beyond what the five senses can process. The texts seek to engage themselves in conversation with this total spectrum of reality. Thus, the role of the worship leader is to listen with one ear to what the text is saying and with another ear to listen to what the community is saying, to have one eye focused in on the text and one eye scanning the signs and sights on the horizon of the community so that the text will be fixed in the liturgical action *on the horizon of the community* and will become a mode by which God will speak God's Word for that community *now*. Following a service with a number of expressions that were crafted to recontextualize a biblical passage, one pastor commented, "It was as though that passage of Scripture was being created here." Such an experience is the goal of liturgical interpretation.

Each community is unique in its engagement with the Word of God. Liturgiologists are discovering more and more the variety of expressions Christian liturgy has developed in each locale, even from the beginning of the church's life. "The history of liturgical practice," Gordon Lathrop reminds us, "has not been a history of steady decline from an original uniformity into a malformed diversity. Rather, Christian assemblies have been marked by diversity from the beginning. The customs attributed to John and Polycarp and the Christians in Asia were different from the customs attributed to the succession of presbyters in the Roman church."[3] We might add that the worship customs in one congregation may be quite different from the worship customs in the church down the street, even though they both may wear the same denominational label.

Hence, to Lathrop, the local " 'assembly' constitutes the most basic symbol of Christian worship."[4] In other ecclesiologies the "congregation" is named as the primary setting of the church and includes the inherent right of the congregation to develop its own liturgical practices. Following the vernacularization of the Roman Catholic mass by the Second Vatican Council, efforts were directed to reach out to the various cultures and to *adapt* local expressions to fit into the Roman rite. More recently, Senn reports, "increasingly adaptation has been replaced by inculturation in which local forms replace the Roman archetype."[5] Worship, for better or worse, for richer or poorer, regardless of the denominational traditions and despite ecclesiastical regulations, is congregationally flavored.

As former Euro-American churches seek to become more multiracial and multicultural through their outreach work, worship increasingly will reflect the uniquenesses of each community and the rich traditions each congregation brings to the worship event. We have seen, especially in former missionary settings in Third World countries, when European-American denominations have sought to translate their liturgies into the native languages and to adapt local customs to fit their worship rituals, congregations are stagnant in their growth. Some even have died out. On the other hand where local congregations were invited and encouraged to develop their own liturgical practices, those communities continue to grow, and their worship life is rich and vibrant. In my role as regional Conference Minister I have seen the transformation that has occurred as indigenous racial and ethnic congregations have been adopted into the wider *koinonia* of the United Church of Christ. Although it is difficult for us Pennsylvania Germans to learn to clap in worship, even to clap off the beat, the worship diversity that the ethnic and racial congregations has brought to the whole church has enriched us all!

There is an ever-present danger, however, that localization can lead to a liturgical sectarianism with each congregation "doing its own thing" or, worse, doing its leader's "own thing." In my role as Conference Minister I have endured one-too-many worship experiences that in form and content had little resemblance to Christian worship in the ecumenical and catholic perspective I have been attempting to develop in this book. Within the diversity that has occurred as each community seeks faithfully to be engaged by God in its conversation with the Word of God, there also is a need to be in conversation with other communities both within the denominational family and within the ecumenical church and other faith communities. Worship rests at the fulcrum, to use Lathrop's definitions, of "local assembly" on the one side and "universal communion" on the other side.[6]

Leaders and congregations sensitive to this delicate balance will discover, in Lathrop's words that "the communion of the churches thus calls the local assembly toward authentic and faithful local witness. And the faithful local assembly gives expression to the catholic character of the church."[7] A faithfulness to pattern worship according to the shape of the divine-human interaction as witnessed to in the Scriptures coupled with a willingness to allow the texts of Scripture appointed in the *Revised Common Lectionary* to become the common sources for each congregation's encounter with the Word of God in worship will help maintain the crucial balance between the local and universal.

The Art of Transposition

Borrowing a term from the catalogue of musical disciplines, I maintain that interpreting biblical texts liturgically involves the *art of transposition*. Much has been written about transposing texts for preaching in general — and primarily with respect to the crafting of sermons — but precious little has been done regarding the transposition of texts *liturgically*. My thesis is that we can utilize the same principles involved in transposing texts in sermon preparation in the task of transposing texts into liturgical expressions. And to ensure that the whole of the worship event may be a common experience, the homiletical and liturgical expressions need to become transpositions of *the same texts*. Therefore, we can overhear Paul Wilson approaching the crafting of a sermon with ears attuned to liturgical transpositions:

> In music, transposing involves writing or playing in a different key from the one designated in the musical score. Here [in preparing a sermon], we are similarly after a change of key: the connection of the original (the concern of the text) with the transposed version (the concern of the sermon/homily) cannot be lost. The tune must be the same since the concern of the sermon/homily can only derive its authority from the text.[8]

So each liturgical expression in a worship service, each prayer, each response, each hymn, becomes a transposition of the text in its new context and, if crafted carefully, will retain a recognizable connection with the shapes and contours of the text. The expression, though in a different context, will sound like the original and become a means by which the worshiper may be put in touch with the Word of God witnessed to in the text itself.

Liturgical transposition therefore is an art inasmuch as it employs principles that are more poetic and musical than scientific. It takes a certain liturgical imagination to interpret a text that appears in the Bible in one genre (story, poetry, song, narrative, etc.) and to transpose it in a different genre (unison prayer, responsive dialogue, hymn, statement of faith, etc.). Thus the question with which the liturgist/interpreter approaches the crafting of liturgical expressions — substituting for "sermon" in Thomas Long's question — is: "How may the [liturgical expression], in a new setting, say and do what the text says and does in its setting?"[9] Perhaps a further refinement would be: "How may the liturgical expression, in a new setting, *be and do* what the text *is and does* in its setting?" In the words of Paul Ricoeur, "The text must be able . . . to 'decontextualize' itself in such a way that it can be 'recontextualized' in a new situation."[10]

Classic examples of recontextualization occur in the Bible itself. Luke tells us (Luke 4:16ff.) that Jesus — following his temptation in the wilderness and at the beginning of his public ministry — went into the synagogue in Nazareth. He was given the scroll of the prophet Isaiah and he read the passage from Isaiah 61:1–2a, "The Spirit of the Lord is upon me. . . ." In the sheer act of reading this lection in a new context Jesus already was engaging in transposing the text. Then Jesus added the homiletical interpretation: "Today this scripture has been fulfilled in your hearing [literally 'in your ears']" (Luke 4:21). Here in one sentence we have a description of the Bible's own hermeneutical circle. "Today," in this moment in history, "this scripture," an ancient text witnessing to the Word of God, "has been fulfilled in your hearing," as the Word of God is enfleshed in the liturgical action of that assembly's participation in Jesus' proclamation. How many more times in the ensuing months and years of his ministry would Jesus speak the texts of the Hebrew scrolls in the new contexts of his proclamation of the good news of God!

Each time the church sang the texts of the psalms and other spiritual songs in the Bible, each time the community heard again the texts of the Gospels read, each time an assembly in some place where the Good News of Jesus Christ had spread listened to the reading of a letter telling of

God's judgment and grace — each time the texts of what had been passed on to them were recontextualized in a new liturgical setting. And each time the church was engaged by those texts, each time became a moment of experiencing the Word of God anew.

Congregations in the Reformed tradition, following Calvin's direction, were accustomed to restrict their singing to the words of the 150 psalms. In some communities that practice continues today. By the eighteenth century there were some defections in the ranks, the most notable of which was Isaac Watts, who began to affirm that there are texts in addition to the texts of Scripture worthy to praise God. Watts was a master in the art of transposing biblical texts into hymns. His hymn "Jesus Shall Reign Where're the Sun" is a Christological transposition of a text from a prayer for the support of King Solomon in the Hebrew Scriptures (Ps. 72) into an act of sung corporate praise to Christ. The Hebrew scripture text (Ps. 72:5) reads: "May he live while the sun endures, and as long as the moon, throughout all generations." Watt's hymn transposition begins:

> Jesus shall reign where'er the sun
>   does its successive journeys run.
> His kingdom stretch from shore to shore,
>   till moons shall wax and wane no more.

This hymn was included in a collection titled *Psalms of David,* psalm-based poems transposed into a New Testament perspective. Moreover, when this hymn is sung today in the context of the church's mission, particularly coupled with the lectionary texts for the last Sunday of the church year (the Festival of Christ the King or Reign of Christ) as suggested in the Lectionary Index of the *New Century Hymnal,*[11] it becomes another genre through which the community is engaged with the Word of God.

Another psalm that has been transposed into a variety of hymn expressions is Psalm 23. Note the way in which the nineteenth-century British priest and poet Henry Williams Baker wonderfully transposed this familiar psalm:

> The King of love my Shepherd is, whose goodness faileth never;
> I nothing lack if am His and He is mine forever.

> Where streams of living water flow my ransomed soul He leadeth,
> And where the verdant pastures grow, with food celestial feedeth.

Perverse and foolish oft I strayed, but yet in love He sought me,
And on His shoulder gently laid, and home, rejoicing, brought me.

In death's dark vale I fear no ill with Thee, dear Lord, beside me;
Thy rod and staff me comfort still, Thy cross before to guide me.

Thou spreadest a table in my sight, Thy unction grace bestoweth;
And O what transport of delight from Thy pure chalice floweth!

And so through all the length of days Thy goodness faileth never;
Good Shepherd, may I sing Thy praise within Thy house forever.

In the first stanza there is a wonderful juxtaposition of images: "King," generally thought of as power figure, is transfigured by Love into the role of the servant Shepherd who knows and cares for those who belong to the shepherd. By the second stanza we get some hint through the phrases "living water," "ransomed soul," and "food celestial" that the King of Love is the Christ. The imagery of the lamb on the shepherd's shoulder in the third stanza suggests Jesus' parable of the Good Shepherd. In the fourth stanza Baker juxtaposes the Old Testament image of the rod and staff with Christ's cross. The fifth stanza introduces sacramental imagery: The anointing with oil in the psalm becomes the unction of chrism for healing, and the cup that overflows is transposed into the chalice of the eucharist. Finally, in the sixth stanza it is clear that this is a hymn of praise to Christ, the Good Shepherd, for all his saving work.

Transpositions and paraphrases of which these two are examples are not replacements for the scripture texts. Rather, they become liturgical expressions that, juxtaposed with the texts, proclaim the Word of God in another genre. Each of them may be used as a gradual or transitional hymn between the text of the psalms themselves and the New Testament lections on the Sundays when these psalms are appointed in the *Revised Common Lectionary*. Psalm 72 is scheduled for Epiphany all three years coupled with Isaiah 60:1–6 ("Nations shall come to your light and kings to the brightness of your dawn") and the visitation of the Magi in Matthew 2:1–12. It also falls on the Second Sunday of Advent in Year A, coupled with the poem about the peaceable kingdom in Isaiah 11:1–10 and the proclamation of John the Baptist in Matthew 3:1–12. Psalm 23 is scheduled for Easter 4, "Good Shepherd Sunday," all three years; Lent 4 in Year A when Psalm 23 follows the story of the anointing of David as

King (1 Sam. 16:1–13); and as part of the alternate lections for Proper 23 in Year A and Proper 11 in Year B.

These hymn-transpositions intend liturgically in another setting of the Christian community to be and do what the text is and does in its literary setting as Psalm 23 in Scripture. Watts and Baker engaged in a liturgical hermeneutic. The texts of the psalms have been decontextualized from their original setting in the Bible and recontextualized liturgically through the art of transposition into a vocalized and musical act of praise to Christ. Nevertheless, it is clear that the expressions are patterned after the very shape of the scriptural texts on which they are based. They say and do liturgically in hymn form what the biblical text says and does in its literary setting.

Sometimes a scripture text itself, without any change in wording, can be transposed into a liturgical expression. The penitential rites and acts in some traditions include 1 John 1:8–9 as a call to confession: "If we say that we have no sin, we deceive ourselves, and the truth is not in us. If we confess our sins, [God] who is faithful and just will forgive us our sins and cleanse us from all unrighteousness." Even though the words are lifted verbatim from the text of Scripture, the change of genres from a literary text to an oral liturgical exhortation constitutes a transposition. The text of an epistle written to the church in a different world-setting in its transposed genre engages the worshiping community now as God's Word calling a new assembly to repentance.

A variant transposition of the same text may result in a responsorial or litany form, reflecting at the beginning of worship the dialogical nature of liturgy. In such a form the text would appear as follows:

Leader: If we say we have no sin, we deceive ourselves and the truth is not in us.

All: **If we confess our sins, God who is faithful and just**
      will forgive us our sins and cleanse us from all unrighteousness.

(1 John 1:8–9)[12]

Leader: Let us acknowledge to God and one another
      that we have missed the mark God intends for us.

Or, as an assurance of forgiveness verse 9 could be transposed:

Leader: If we confess our sins, God, who is faithful and just will forgive us our
      sins and cleanse us from all unrighteousness.   (1 John 1:9)

Leader: Believe the Good News.

All: **In Jesus Christ we are forgiven!**

The sense of dialogue is heightened if the two "leader" sentences are spoken by two different persons. The variations of shaping liturgical expressions that the Scriptures suggest are many. All it takes is approaching the texts with a certain liturgical imagination. We shall explore some of the methodology involved later.

The particular text from the First Epistle of John is part of the lection appointed for Easter 2 in Year B in the *Revised Common Lectionary*. It can be used as transposed above as a call to penitence or assurance of forgiveness, *and* the lection can be read again in its entirety as one of the Scripture lessons. Repetition is not a deadly liturgical sin! Repeated hearings of the same text in different settings or genres may bring about a welcomed recognition: "Ah, there it is again!" In that moment of awareness not only is the liturgy shaped by the Scripture but also a life is shaped as the Word of God who meets us as the Scripture is fulfilled in our hearing.

The Bible is full of liturgical expressions, as I mentioned earlier, that in their preliterary forms were first experienced in worshiping communities. The New Testament Letters, for example, were intended to be read publicly in the gathered community, and in their oralization became homiletical expressions. When 1 Corinthians 13 is appointed in the *Revised Common Lectionary* (Epiphany 4 in Year C), it may be appropriate for the whole congregation to read it in unison either in pew Bibles or printed worship leaflets. Changing the genre by recontextualizing this passage as a corporate reading can enable the whole congregation to be engaged in an expression of proclamation and help a very familiar text to be encountered in a different way.

Another example is Philippians 2:6–11, a passage that when spoken by the congregation in unison becomes an extraordinary statement of the Christian faith. It may be most helpful to print the text in a form for corporate speech in a worship bulletin or insert. As such the statement may be prefaced with the preceding sentence as an introduction:

Leader: Let the same mind be in you that was in Christ Jesus.

All: **Christ, though he was in the form of God,**
did not regard equality with God as something to be exploited,
but emptied himself, taking the form of a slave,
being born in human likeness.
And being found in human form, he humbled himself
and became obedient to the point of death — even death on a cross.

> Therefore God also highly exalted him
> and gave him the name that is above every name,
> so that at the name of Jesus
> every knee should bend, in heaven and on earth and under the earth,
> and every tongue should confess that Jesus Christ is Lord,
> to the glory of God the Father.   (Phil. 2:5–11, adapt.)

Used in such a way this expression is not meant to be a substitute for the classic creeds, but, on occasions, particularly when this text is appointed (Proper 21 in Year A), it may serve as an alternate statement of faith. In both examples cited the mere act of speaking in unison a literary text is in itself an interpretation of the text. The same can be said of the reading aloud of Scripture in dialogue or even by a single lector. Simply changing the genre from a literary text to an expression in oral speech is a transposition of that text.

Crafting Transpositions

I discovered long ago during my years as a parish pastor with the weekly responsibility of crafting worship services that there are occasions when I could not find an appropriate prayer or other worship expression that seemed to fit with the text. It was this lack of what I needed that prompted me to begin to do my own transpositions. Some of these found their way into the 1987 collection published as *Worship Vessels* and have been revised, along with some new expressions, into the two-volume set *Immersed in the Splendor of God* and *Blessed by the Presence of God*. During the past fifteen years the setting of my ministry has changed, and now I am responsible for crafting liturgies for regional gatherings of the church and particularly for monthly services that are designed particularly to enable parish pastors to worship and to gain some practical insights for their own responsibilities as worship leaders. Each service is based on the texts of the *Revised Common Lectionary* for a Sunday several weeks in advance. Although the communities gathered for these services have changed, I still find the need many times to create my own transpositions of the lectionary texts so that the services will have a sense of unity among the various expressions.

The following is a penitential act from one such service based on the lections for Proper 24 in Year B of the *Revised Common Lectionary:* Isaiah 53:4–12, Hebrews 5:1–10, and Mark 10:35–45. The textual focus for sermon and eucharistic liturgy was Jesus' foretelling of his death and resurrection and the subsequent plea of James and John for a place with Jesus in glory. Their inappropriate request prompted Jesus' teaching about servanthood: "Whoever wishes to become great among you must be your servant, and whoever wishes to be first among you must be slave of all. For the Son of Man came not to be served but to serve, and to give his life a ransom for many" (Mark 10:43–45).

The service began with a call to gather the community transposed verbatim from a complementary text from Philippians 2:10–11:

Leader: At the name of Jesus every knee should bend
           in heaven and on earth and under the earth,
           and every tongue should confess that Jesus Christ is Lord
           to the glory of God the Father.

This complementary text provided a sense of gathering the community that none of the prescribed lections could do. Sometimes it is necessary for the worship leader to decide whether or not it is appropriate to choose an alternative or complementary text to enable the liturgical action to take place and for that action to be structured according to the pattern of the divine-human interaction witnessed to in Scripture and tradition. Yet that other text, like hymns and other worship expressions, must be complementary to the main text around which the liturgy is shaped. Again, such decisions about choosing alternate and complementary texts are part of the process of orchestration that I will discuss in chapter 5. Although the genre of this particular text in the Philippian letter is a statement of faith, here I transposed it into a call to worship without really changing the words themselves. I felt this text, spoken verbatim, powerfully could be and do in this new setting what it is and does in its original setting in the Bible and would serve to gather the community into worship.

This call to worship was followed by the singing of four stanzas of Charles Wesley's familiar hymn of praise to the risen and ascended Christ: "Ye Servants of God...." The fourth stanza continues to call the community to worship with images from the book of Revelation:

> **"Salvation to God, who sits on the throne,"**
> **let all cry aloud, and honor the Son;**
> **The praises of Jesus the angels proclaim,**
> **fall down on their faces and worship the Lamb.**

In the Gospel lesson on which this service is based the disciples ask for the privilege of being in a special place of honor with Jesus when he comes into his glory. That same human desire is baggage we all still carry with us into our meeting with Christ. Therefore, it was appropriate, I felt, for us to come to Christ at the beginning of this worship event acknowledging that Christ is risen and ascended into his glory and with the almost unconscious desire that we too might have the opportunity to be with him at his right hand.

Yet in the presence of the Lamb upon the throne, the awareness dawns on us that there is a certain self-serving motivating this coziness with Christ. In the mode of God's self-disclosure in the Scriptures, as I indicated in the discussion of structure in the previous chapter, there is that moment of awareness that there is a disjuncture between divine and human ways. So I chose to bridge into the act of confession of sin with another complementary text, in J. B. Phillips's paraphrase, taken from the same discussion about Christ's high priestly role in Hebrews which is the theme of the Epistle lesson appointed for this Sunday:

Leader: Seeing that we have a great High Priest
           who has entered the inmost heaven, Jesus the Son of God,

People: **Let us therefore approach the throne of grace with fullest confidence,**
           that we may receive mercy for our failures
           and grace to help in the hour of need.   (Heb. 4:14, 16, Phillips, adapt.)

The Gospel lesson is foreshadowed in the prayer of confession. I took the themes of the Gospel text and transposed them into a prayer of confession in which the worshipers acknowledge the same things. This prayer, of course, was prayed *before* the text of Gospel was read later in the service. Yet it links the act of penitence to the hearing of the Word, thus weaving these two acts into an organic union arising out of the text itself.

Leader: Let us pray.

All: **Lord Jesus Christ, we come to you with deep needs**
           and great expectations.
           We need communion with you.
           We need to be touched with sacred things that sign your presence
           and signify our oneness with you.
           In spending ourselves to serve you
           we find the springs of spirituality running dry.

> So we expect you to do for us what we yearn for most —
>> to sit at table with you and to be fed with more than bread,
>> and to be satisfied with more than wine.
> Yet in our craving to linger long with you at this table
>> we may fail to follow you as you arise to go ahead of us;
>> we may miss finding you in the form of a slave,
>> or meeting you again in the guise of a gardener.
> Lord Jesus Christ, we know we will miss the mark you intend for us,
>> so we ask for a prevenient forgiveness.

Leader: Lord, have mercy on us.

All: **Christ, have mercy on us.**

Leader: Lord, have mercy on us, and grant us your peace. Amen.

silence

Leader: Jesus promised: "Ask, and it will be given you; search, and you will find; knock, and the door will be opened for you." (Matt. 7:7) Therefore I announce that in Jesus Christ we are forgiven.

All: **Amen.**

Response: *in unison; the congregation may stand.* HANOVER

> **Then let us adore, and give him his right,**
>> **all glory and power, all wisdom and might,**
> **All honor and blessing, with angels above,**
>> **and thanks never ceasing, and infinite love.**

Note in the prayer how I attempted to allow the life-texts of this community of pastors ("Lord, Jesus Christ, we come to you with deep needs and great expectations . . . so we expect you to do for us what we yearn for most") to be juxtaposed with the images of the Gospel text ("James and John . . . came forward to him and said to him, 'Teacher, we want you to do for us whatever we ask of you.'"). Note also how the request of James and John in the text ("Grant us to sit, one at your right hand and one at your left, in your glory") is transposed into a petition to be with Christ in the eucharist ("to sit at table with you and to be fed with more than bread . . ."). Finally, in Jesus' saying, ". . . whoever wishes to be first among you must be slave of all," the "slave" is reimaged as Christ himself: "we may miss finding you in the form of a slave, or meeting you again in the guise of a gardener." Obviously, the final image is that of the Christ whom Mary confused with the gardener on the day of resurrection (John

20:15). We come to Christ wanting an at-one-ness in which we hope to linger long, yet Jesus' desire for himself and for us is servanthood. The Gospel has a way of boomeranging on our desires and intentions, and most often we do not really recognize the Christ who is already among us in the form of a servant.

The act concluded with another complementary text: words of forgiveness transposed verbatim from Jesus' saying, "Ask, and it will be given you..." (Matt. 7:7, Luke 11:9) and the final doxological stanza of Wesley's hymn with which the service had begun. Singing stanzas of hymns in this fashion as a kind of framework around the spoken expressions links them in a unified whole. Sometimes, depending on the nature of the hymn text, the service may begin with the singing of one or more stanzas and close with other stanzas of the same hymn. In this particular service the final stanza of the gathering hymn brought the introductory part of the service to a close.

It is in crafting the expressions for the celebration of the eucharist that worship leaders feel most uneasy about departing from the words printed in hymnals and worship books. Obviously these authorized liturgies should serve as the foundational liturgies not only for the services of Holy Communion but also for the whole service of Word and Sacrament. However, there are times when, to allow the worship service to be shaped into an organic and unified whole, the Scriptures may prompt other wordings of the eucharistic liturgy. The structure of the eucharistic event remains the same; only the wordings and expressions change. One of the uniquenesses of the *Book of Common Worship* prepared by the Theology and Worship Ministry Unit for the Presbyterian Church (U.S.A.) and the Cumberland Presbyterian Church is that it includes a thorough collection of worship resources, including variants of the eucharistic prayers, for the various festivals and seasons of the church year according to the *Common Lectionary*.[13]

If the worship leader understands the fourfold structure ("take," "bless," "break," and "give") that emerges from Scripture and tradition and heeds the caution that James White gave regarding liturgical experimentation, she or he is free to allow the Scriptures to shape the expressions that will be indigenous to a particular celebration of the eucharist. Again, the purpose of such transposition is to allow the text to say and do in this setting — namely, in the words and actions of the eucharist — what it said and did in its setting in the Bible.

The following communion liturgy was part of the same service for Proper 24 in Year B that we considered above. The prayer of confession expressed the desire to Christ to sit with him at eucharist. Again the same text prompted my transposing the disciples' easy answer to Jesus, "We are able," into a prayer of humble access in which the worshipers petition Christ, "We come to your table not because we are able...rather, to do eucharist...." The transposition took the following shape as a liturgical expression for the celebration of Holy Communion:

Pastor: Lift up your hearts!

All: We lift them up to the Lord!

Pastor: Lord Jesus Christ, you came not to be served
           but to serve, and to give your life a ransom for many.

All: We come to your table not because we are able
           to drink the cup you drank
           nor to be baptized with the suffering you received.
           We come, rather, to do eucharist, to give you thanks
           for pouring out your own life for us,
           and to share in the life-giving food and drink
           you serve to us in this holy meal.

Pastor: In the beginning you were the eternal Word with God
           through whom all things were made.
           In you was life and the light of all people.
           In the fullness of time you were born in human likeness
           and lived as one of us.
           In self-giving love you emptied yourself
           and took upon yourself the form of a slave
           to bear all humanity in your own body — even to the cross.
           Through your resurrection you triumphed over the powers of sin
           and death
           and opened the heavenly realm to all who live and die in you.
           You promised that we would never be left alone in this world as
           orphaned ones but would be given the Holy Spirit to comfort us
           and to empower us to be your witnesses to the ends of the earth.
           We hold sacred those faithful women and men who have accepted the
           cost and joy of discipleship to be your servants in the service of others.
           In thanksgiving we remember them and name them before you: *name(s)*
           Surrounded at this table by your faithful ones in heaven and on earth,
           we join our voices with them to sing your praise:

All:

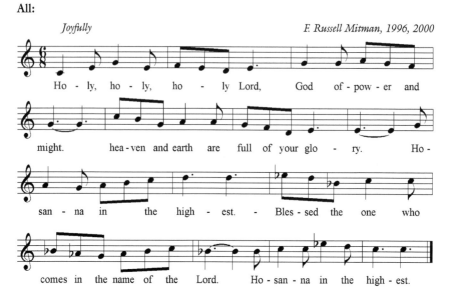

Joyfully   F. Russell Mitman, 1996, 2000

Ho - ly, ho - ly, ho - ly Lord, God of - pow - er and might. hea - ven and earth are full of your glo - ry. Ho - san - na in the high - est. - Bles - sed the one who comes in the name of the Lord. Ho - san - na in the high - est.

All: We offer these gifts from the earth
          together with the thanksgiving of our lives and service.
       Through your Holy Spirit transform these ordinary things
          that they may be to us sacred signs
          whereby we may know you in the breaking of this bread
          and the sharing of this cup.
       Unite us at this table in communion with all your servant-saints
          until one day we all shall feast together
          at the great banquet table of heaven. Amen.

The words of institution coupled with the breaking of the bread and pouring the wine follow, and the prayer is completed with the Lord's Prayer. Following communion the congregation prays in unison the prayer of thanksgiving:

       We thank you, Lord Jesus, for feeding us at this table
          with the sacred signs that point us to the mystery
             of your servant love for all humanity.
       As you came not to be served but to serve and to give yourself,
          empower us for a servant ministry as your prophets and priests
          in your name and in the service of all your people. Amen.

Note how the imagery of the text like a theme of a musical fugue repeats itself several times in the prayers before and following the meal.

Since this text focuses on servanthood, I crafted time in the eucharistic prayer for the worshipers individually to name aloud the persons who exemplify servant discipleship to them and to join with them in spirit in singing Christ's praise. The setting of the traditional Sanctus-Benedictus ("Holy, holy, holy") is one I composed to express the eucharistic joy that is experienced in the communion of the saints. It may be accompanied by keyboard, guitar, drums, maracas, and other rhythm instruments — perhaps even dance! The keyboard accompaniment may be found on p. 164. Although this eucharistic prayer is addressed to Christ, the Second Person of the Trinity, it, like most traditional forms of the Great prayer, is Trinitarian in character. Moreover the Sanctus, a third-century transposition of Isaiah 6:3 and Revelation 4:8, joined with the Benedictus ("blessed is he who comes" from Ps. 118:26, chanted by the crowd during Jesus' entry into Jerusalem in Matt. 21:9) in its traditional setting within the eucharistic prayer is interpreted Christologically: *Christ* is the blessed "One who comes in the name of the Lord."

Hippolytus, a presbyter in Rome around the turn of the third century, said in relation to eucharistic prayer that "it is not at all necessary to recite the same words we have prescribed... in giving thanks to God, but let each one pray according to his ability,... only let him pray what is right worship [*orthodoxia*]."[14] *Orthodoxia* in a contemporary interpretation may be construed as worship that is patterned after the structure that is shaped after the very nature of the divine-human interaction witnessed to in the Scriptures and that has found ecumenical concurrence today as outlined in the previous chapter. To Hippolytus, knowing what was *orthodoxia* permitted the worship leader to be free with the text of the eucharistic prayer. In our own time James White said, "Once one has mastered the basic form of eucharistic prayers, it is possible to improvise them in as many different ways as one can write sonnets in the specified form."[15]

Note finally that the expressions, shaped by the Gospel lesson and the complementary text from Philippians with which the service began, were integrally related to those that formed the liturgy for the eucharist and the conclusion of the service. The organic nature of this liturgy was the result of a common text, complemented by other texts, coming to expression in a variety of liturgical genres, including the sermon. By the way, the title of the sermon based on Jesus' question in this same text, "What is it you want me to do for you?" was "Customer Satisfaction." The sample worship expressions I have included here illustrate how one text can shape several different kinds of transpositions.

There are many modes for the transposition of texts into liturgical acts. In one of my visitations to a local church I discovered that the pastor had crafted a liturgy with some wonderful expressions that resonated harmoniously with the sermon I was preaching. I complimented him following the service and asked, "Did you write the prayers of confession and thanksgiving?" He said, "No, but I know where to look for them." Transposing biblical texts to create an organic liturgy does not necessarily mean that one has to create each expression from scratch. The secret lies sometimes in finding the suitable transpositions in the many anthologies of worship resources that are available in the same way that one searches for the hymns that fit best the biblical texts.

Both this pastor and I had started from the *Revised Common Lectionary* texts for that particular Sunday, and, although each of us had worked independently to prepare our own parts of that worship service, together we enabled an organic liturgy to take shape in that congregation's worship hour. Immediately both of us — and hopefully the congregation also — became aware of how what each of us had prepared separately complemented each other and enabled a corporate experience to occur. Organic liturgy is possible in prayer-book churches, in free-church traditions, and in predominately oral worship settings where there is need for little or nothing at all to be printed in order for an integrated liturgical action to take place. The same principles are operative regardless of the modes of transposition. All it takes is a touch of liturgical and homiletical imagination on the part of the worship leader.

Imagination is a gift of God that is given to everyone, not in equal measure, yet a given that each person has. Unfortunately the training we have received at the hands of a left-over Enlightenment pedagogy has suppressed the imagination in most adults. Younger children still possess it in fuller measure. I suggest that as worship leaders we spend time with children to unlearn our bad habits of mind and to rediscover the gift that God has given us. Walter Brueggemann has said,

> The community waits for the text that may be a tent for the spirit.
> ...But if the text is to claim authority it will require neither the
> close reasoning of a canon lawyer, nor the precision of a technician,
> but it will require an artist to render the text in quite fresh ways,

so that the text breaks life open among the baptized as it never has before.[16]

The audience for Brueggemann's words is preachers, and the context is preaching. Let us, as I believe he would allow us, widen again the word "preaching" to "proclamation," and let it be inclusive of all of worship. From such a perspective we continue listening to Brueggemann when he says, "I want to consider preaching as a poetic construal of an alternative world."[17] The idea that the role of the prophet is to provide an alternative to the principalities and powers is classic Brueggemann. Let us envision not only how preaching but also orchestrating *all of worship* involves the "poetic construal of an alternative world" in a community, in Brueggemann's words, "that has come all too often to expect nothing but prose."[18] Again, the context for his remarks is preaching, but we can interpret them in a liturgical perspective as well and say with him that all of worship is "an artistic moment in which the words are concrete but open, close to our life but moving out to new angles of reality."

A Place to Begin

Transposing begins with simply spending time with the appointed texts. Twenty minutes a day is suggested by some. This will be a time of prayer and discernment to allow the texts to raise questions about themselves, about the interpreter, about the community, and even the world. Note that I did not say, "Start by reading the commentaries." They may or may not be helpful to the interpretive task, but their role is secondary. The primary mode is reading and living with the text for several days, perhaps in several different translations, maybe even in the biblical languages themselves.

No one worship service generally will be able to encompass all of the texts, so a process of narrowing the focus begins to center the transposer's homiletical and liturgical imagination on one text or even a part of a text that will become the primary text. The other appointed texts may serve to complement the one that becomes the primary text, although it is difficult sometimes during the season after Pentecost for those who use the alternate semicontinuous readings to see the common thread. Moreover, these same texts will come around again in three years; there is no need to fear becoming repetitious. Furthermore, it would be marvelously affirming if someone in the congregation remembered enough to say, "But, Pastor, you said that three years ago!"

There is no prescribed methodology for this selection except to say that the focusing on the primary text or portion of a text is something that emerges during the twenty-minute-a-day sessions. Discernment is a spiritual exercise and discipline that participates in the very mystery of God. God has yet more truth and light to break forth from God's holy Word, and God will highlight the text with God's own pen! Prayer and meditation are the ancient tools of discernment. So also is reading the texts aloud individually or with colleagues or a study group in the congregation. When we read Scripture aloud, the Word begins to emerge from the words, and that Word will drive the focusing lens of the imagination and become the integrating power that will shape sermon and liturgy. However, the twenty-minute stay with the texts cannot begin on Saturday evening! The primary text will emerge if we start early enough — and "early" may mean months in advance!

And after a while the text will begin to challenge the cultural assumptions that the interpreter and the community bring to the text. The Bible is the church's book, and the Word of God is for the community and arises in the community of faith. When I was a parish pastor I met at least an hour and a half each Tuesday with groups from the congregation. We prayed and read the texts together, and all at once new insights began to arise that were the seeds not only for the next Sunday's sermon and liturgy but also of the alternative world that the texts were beginning to construe for us in our engagement with them. When someone reads and others hear "The kingdom of heaven is like . . . ," already the text is beginning to create an alternative view of reality that is connected parabolically with people's experience *in* this world yet finds its origins and authority in realities that are not *of* this world.

I begin the crafting of liturgy and sermon by typing the words of the text at the top of my computer screen followed by a diagram, modified from a format suggested by Professor Paul Scott Wilson,[19] showing the connecting concerns of text on the one hand and the concern of the transposition of the text into sermon and liturgy on the other hand. Thus, I am conjoining the homiletical and liturgical tasks through a common hermeneutical approach, and I begin to compose both sermon and liturgy simultaneously. I create two fields, one labeled "sermon," and the other "liturgy," and as ideas and words and phrases arise in my imagination, I list them under each of the headings. Sometimes my reflecting on the text evokes the words of a hymn or a phrase that is the kernel of a prayer or sparks the recollection of some liturgical expression from the tradition or of something that I crafted for a previous service.

Even the structure or order of the worship expressions begins to emerge. I list all these under the "liturgy" heading. Similarly under the "sermon" heading I type in double-spaced lines the words and phrases that emerge and that later I will arrange in a progression and expand into the sentences and paragraphs of the sermon. Thus, both sermon and liturgy begin literally to write themselves simultaneously, and the eventual shapes both the sermon and the liturgy will take begin to be patterned according to the inherent structure of the text itself. For example, the lectionary Gospel text for All Saints Day (or the First Sunday in November) in Year B according to the *Revised Common Lectionary* is the story of the raising of Lazarus (John 11:32–44). In crafting a sermon and liturgy for a worship service for parish pastors, I entered the text at the top of the page on my computer screen:

> **Jesus said, "Take away the stone. . . ." When he had said this, he cried out with a loud voice, "Lazarus, come out!"**

Then beneath the text, after I had determined the direction the text was leading, I entered the following, according to Professor Wilson's format:

Concern of the Text: Jesus calls Lazarus out of the tomb.
Concern of the Worship: Jesus calls us from death to life.

With one eye of the imagination on the text and the other visualizing the assembly of pastors and the concerns with which they would be gathering for this service, as I journaled my reflections under the categories of "sermon" and "liturgy" I added in words, phrases, the first lines of possible hymns, prayer fragments, special emphases, and whatever emerged from my session of engagement with the text. These electronic jottings I expanded later into the specific liturgical expressions — prayers, sermon, hymns, and other worship acts — that eventually emerged in the ordered sequence of a liturgy for this particular day in the church year (see page 111).

First, I transposed the Gospel text, which is a narrative of what happened when Jesus arrived at Lazarus's tomb, into a corporate prayer of confession and coupled it with the traditional Kyrie, in this case spoken in unison, followed by periods of programmed silence:

> O God of Martha and Lazarus and of all the saints
> who have proclaimed that Jesus Christ is Lord,
>   we come to you in the poverty of our own profession.
> There have been those opportunities to minister that we have avoided
> and occasions to bring healing that we have passed by.
> In the tombs of our own vulnerabilities we stay bound to the past
> and chained to the routines we find most comfortable.
> The remembrances of "if only I had been there" haunt us to tears
> and mark with pain the sins of whatever we have left undone.
>
> > Lord, have mercy on us.   *silence*
> > Christ, have mercy on us.   *silence*
> > Lord, have mercy on us.   *silence*

The appointed Epistle in the same set of lections is Revelation 21:1–6a, a portion of which I transposed into a call to worship in the following form:

> Leader: Behold, the home of God is among mortals.
>   God will dwell with them as their God; they will be God's people,
>   and God will be with them and be their God.
>   God will wipe every tear from their eyes.
>   Death will be no more; mourning and crying and pain will be no more,
>   for the former things have passed away.   (Rev. 21:3b–4, alt.)

This call to worship also could be prefaced with another voice, reading verses 1 to 3a: "Then I saw a new heaven and a new earth, for the first heaven and the first earth had passed away...and I heard a loud voice from the throne saying." If the words were read by a male voice, it would be appropriate for the second leader's words, "Behold, the home of God is among mortals,..." to be spoken by a female voice. Verses 3b–4, as translated by the NRSV, is set as poetry, while verses 1–3a are blocked as prose. There are many variant texts of the poetry section suggesting that this many be one of those liturgical expressions of the early church that eventually was incorporated into the text by the writer of the Apocalypse.

If, as Walter Brueggemann says, as cited above, preaching — and I add worship also — becomes the "poetic construal of an alternative world," to begin a worship service with the firm announcement, "Then I saw a *new* heaven and a *new* earth," is to allow this ancient text in another setting of the church's life to invite a congregation to step into the new reality that God is opening now in that very homiletical and liturgical moment. The texts are not being read — or explained — as history and science but are spoken poetically and prophetically as the proclamation of God's new doing. God is speaking from the throne, inviting and ushering the ones redeemed in Christ to step into the alternative world that God is preparing before their very eyes — theologically, that is, not ophthalmologically. We dare not be timid to speak for God when we proclaim the words of Scripture that by God's doing may become — in that moment of articulation and hearing — God's own Word!

Conceiving Metaphorically

Much of the language in the transpositions we have just considered, like the Scriptures from which they emerged, is metaphoric. Even my one-sentence identification of the homiletic and liturgical concern of this service is metaphoric: "Jesus calls us from death to life." Obviously "death" and "life" here are not biological terms describing the natural world. They are metaphors for the "death" that occurs when we are "buried in baptism" — another Pauline metaphor — and the "life" that Christ gives by virtue of his death and resurrection. As in all metaphors, the terms are reversed from the natural order: Death precedes life, or, life comes after death. It is saying — like the "born again" words in Jesus' reply to Nicodemus — that what appears to be impossible at one level of meaning is true at a deeper level.

The word "metaphor" comes from Greek stems that mean "to carry over" from one thing to another. Metaphors are different from similes in that they do not include the words "like" or "as." Similes are one-to-one comparisons: The psalmist cries, "As a deer longs for flowing streams, so my soul longs for you, O God" (Ps. 42:1). Metaphors, on the other hand, invite a crossing over of meanings: Jesus said, "I am the bread of life" (John 6:35). Moreover, metaphors, unlike similes, are multivalent: "death" and "life" have many layers of meaning simultaneously.

To proclaim the words of the Apocalypse, in the example above, that the "former things have passed away" to people struggling against the principalities and powers of a consumer-secular society is to invite them metaphorically into the reality that in the reign of God Caesar no longer is Lord. Rodney Kennedy explains:

The metaphors of the New Testament [are] disclosers of possibilities for human existence which seem and are beyond the limit of what our ordinary language and experience might imagine. I do not mean that religious metaphors present a new, supernatural world wherein we may escape the world in which we live. I do mean that metaphor *redescribes* ordinary reality in order to *disclose* a *new,* and extraordinary possibility for our lives.[20]

The Bible is full of metaphors, some of which may have originated in preliterary forms as liturgical expressions. According to Gail Ramshaw, "Christian liturgy is the communal celebration of biblical metaphors."[21] She says,

In the liturgy not any old metaphor, or any new metaphor, will do. Liturgy is not an individual's performance laid before others; nor is it a collection of texts of self-expression. Liturgical language takes as its model not a Pulitzer prize–winning poem but the prologue of John: it is speech that the baptized community already shares. Liturgical language bonds together the worshiping people because it is already their speech. Liturgical metaphors change over the decades. The texts, hymns, and prayers have evolved over the centuries and must continue to evolve. But innovations in liturgical speech must take care that novel metaphors not fragment the assembly but unite it. Liturgical imagery is not idiosyncratic but communal.[22]

In another essay Ramshaw explores the issue of inclusivity in relation to metaphors with respect to liturgical language: "Liturgy includes the communal recitation of the central metaphors of the faith, but liturgy is grounded in the assembly. . . . The liturgy is the expression of all the people of God, and all those people need to have their voices heard."[23] Hence, consistent with the title of the essay, *Liturgical Language: Keeping it Metaphoric, Making it Inclusive,* she asks:

How can the liturgical language of our assemblies be both metaphorical and inclusive? How can the language pour down past centuries of Christian imagination and also spring up to articulate contemporary needs? . . . Some people lean too far toward metaphor, not very concerned that all voices be heard; others lean too far towards inclusivity, unable to program their computers to produce metaphors and accustomed to the flattened babble of E-mail.[24]

Crafting worship expressions amid the wars in both culture and church over inclusive language involves a deep sensitivity to this delicate balance. There are many voices speaking from many perspectives on this issue and offering differing canons as to what is currently appropriate liturgical language. I do not wish to be drawn into the debates arising among the various "isms" that have emerged from experience-based theological constructs. Gail Ramshaw's dictum, "keep it metaphoric, make it inclusive," can be a helpful guide to all of us with responsibility for crafting and orchestrating liturgy. It is also humbling to be reminded that in our attempts to be justly inclusive we can become simultaneously unjustly exclusive. All of us have been forced to endure prayers telling God what is politically correct for God and us to do. On the other hand, we also have suffered through homiletical and liturgical metaphors piled upon each other to the point that the Scriptures and their transpositions end up in a maze of allegories through which the worshipers need a map of rubrics to find their way. I tend to think that in mainline Protestantism the former is more prevalent than the latter.

The following penitential prayer is based on the Epistle lection for Proper 14 in Year B of the *Revised Common Lectionary*. The focused text for this transposition as well as for the sermon that I entitled "Graceful Words" was the following from the Letter to the Ephesians:

> Let no evil talk come out of your mouths, but only what is useful for building up, as there is need, so that your words may give grace to those who hear. (Eph. 4:29)

Note the metaphors and the juxtaposition of "Word" and "words" in the transposition of the text into a prayer:

> O God, whose Word was in the beginning of creation
> and became flesh in Jesus Christ:
> We confess that sometimes we are careless with human words —
> words that are spoken quickly,
> yet have such lasting effects,
> words that spill easily in anger from our lips,
> yet wound deeply those on whom they fall,

> words that wear pleasant outward faces
>> yet disguise less than benign inward intents,
> words that come cheaply in anonymity,
>> yet cost dearly in human intimacy,
> words that promise faithfully in adversity,
>> yet forget unconsciously in prosperity.
> O God whose Word is both judgment and grace,
>> tell us the ways our words can hurt,
>>> but speak to us also the saving Word that heals. Amen.

silence

The purpose of any prayer of confession is to acknowledge the theological and ethical disjuncture between God and us: Our words are not God's Word; our ways are not God's ways. "Word" is a theological metaphor that confronts our flattened, e-mail-like words, with judgment and grace. Something of the human dilemma is verbalized in the prayer of confession just cited through the comparisons of "quickly"/ "lasting," "spill easily"/"wound deeply," "come cheaply"/"cost dearly," "promise faithfully"/"forget unconsciously." Obviously words in a strictly descriptive sense do not "wear pleasant outward faces," yet the metaphor crosses meaning over so that we can say, yes, words do indeed sometimes "wear pleasant outward faces, yet disguise less than benign inward intents," for we all *have experienced* the painful consequences of what those pleasant-faced words conceal. This is our confession to God and to one another.

Writing Orally

Crafting liturgy also involves writing in an oral style. We tend to think that "oral" and "literary" are opposites: One is spoken; the other written. Yet in composing liturgical expressions, the worship leader needs to think and write in a primarily oral style because the intent of the orchestration is to enable the congregation to engage in corporate speech rather than in private silent reading. The Psalms, in their literary forms in the Bible, reflect that they were and still are primarily oral expressions meant to be said or sung corporately. One of the persistent problems that I note in some leaders' transpositions is that they are written essentially in literary forms. Often these expressions then are printed in worship bulletins and leaflets with the intention that the congregation will speak them aloud.

Some are wonderful expressions of the faith with a depth of pathos and even sometimes a touch of poetry. Yet when these words are spoken in unison, the assembly stumbles over them. We shall speak more about oral communication in the next chapter; however, it is critical that the composer is fully aware in the crafting of expressions *before* they are printed that they will be spoken by a liturgist, homilist, or the congregation as a whole. Regarding preaching Paul Scott Wilson says:

> After often eighteen years of academic training for ministry, most of it for the page, our theological writing tends not to imitate speech; rather, our theological speech normally imitates writing. Speech that imitates academic writing often sounds like a lecture, or an essay being read.... Once we conceive of preaching as an oral event, we begin to shift our ways of thinking. Instead of composing with the eye for the page, we begin to compose with the ear for oral delivery and aural reception, attentive to various needs of the listeners.[25]

I maintain that what Wilson is saying about preaching also applies to the crafting of all expressions in the liturgy. As I compose on the word processor and see the words emerging on the video monitor, I speak them aloud, often changing words as I am speaking them so that later they can be spoken and heard orally in sermon and liturgy. After years of being exposed to this practice my family has begun to overlook that Dad is in his study talking to himself again!

Note, for instance, the way in which the following prayer of thanksgiving is written and printed to facilitate oral speech. It is based on the familiar story of Joseph's dream in Matthew 1:18–25 that is the Gospel lection for the Fourth Sunday in Advent in Year A.

Leader: As we approach the sacred Eve, O God,
  you have filled us with the holy mysteries that prepare us for your coming.
  Nourish in us a readiness to cradle your Incarnation,
  and give birth in us a trust
  that will take us beyond Bethlehem by another way
  and will lead to a new day of justice and peace for all humankind.

People: Amen. Come, Lord Jesus!

Scripting Rhetorically

Composing worship expressions not only involves writing orally but also preparing the script for the liturgical action with an eye to rhetoric. "Rhetoric" is a word that has either dropped out of most homiletical and liturgical lexicons or has received negative press as showy or overelaborate discourse. "Cut the rhetoric!" has been added to the collection that also includes "Don't preach to me!" Yet rhetoric is an ancient art that every Greek citizen needed to learn. Since no lawyers were permitted to speak for their clients in court and there were no judges to rule, citizens needed to have the oral skills to *persuade* the jury of the validity of their cases. Aristotle's *Rhetoric* was the basic text. Essentially in his construct any persuasive speech involved (1) *ethos,* the personal character of the speaker; (2) *pathos,* the emotional appeal aiming at putting the audience in a certain frame of mind; and (3) *logos,* the logical argument aiming at proof. The order is Aristotle's, and it is interesting the he placed *ethos,* the personal character of the speaker, first and *logos,* the logical argument, last. Since the Enlightenment Western culture in general and preaching in particular have reversed Aristotle's order.

Recently there has been a rediscovery of rhetoric's place in preaching. Paul Wilson writes:

> We conceive of preaching as the event of God meeting us. A sermon, conceived in this manner, is not merely words. Our words do things. God uses them and acts through them to bring forth God's purposes.... An understanding of preaching as God's event affects not only the words we choose and oral ways of thought, but also how we communicate.... We return to the classical roots of preaching, and join with others in approaching it in part as rhetoric. While preaching is unique, not least by being God's word, it is closely related to rhetoric as conversation or dialogue whose aim is persuasion or identification that seeks to enroll people in a way of life.[26]

Again, he is writing about preaching sermons. However, what he is urging in the homiletical discipline is also true with regard to the liturgical task. Translated liturgically the question becomes: How do worship leaders communicate persuasively in the enactment of liturgy? Obviously the goal is not to draw attention to the leader nor to prove what the leader is saying, even about God, but to allow the Word of God to affect the community with God's own judgment and grace.

Wilson also addresses the possible reservations that some may have about the issue of persuasion and the place of rhetoric in theology and homiletics, namely, on the one side, that the purpose of preaching is to proclaim, not to persuade, and on the other side that the role of modern rhetoric is not to persuade people of only one point of view but to deconstruct reality and to emphasize plurality, ambiguity, and choice. He concludes:

> We do not preach a text in the first instance, deconstructed or reconstructed; we preach Jesus Christ, crucified and risen, as he encounters us through the Holy Spirit and in the church. Our rhetoric is in Christ's service. . . . What is avoidable and should be avoided is bad manipulation, unfaithful persuasion, that which takes advantage of our hearers. Moreover, the Holy Spirit needs our offering with which to work.[27]

The issue of rhetoric, although it is very much a part of *doing* liturgy which is the subject of chapter 6, is raised here because it is integral also to the composing of worship expressions and the orchestration of liturgy that we will address in the next chapter. Long before leaders enter chancel and pulpit the persuasive powers of *ethos, pathos,* and *logos* need to be *written into* the forms and expressions that will be part of the worship event. Otherwise liturgy will revert easily to the prosaic and, in Gail Ramshaw's insightful metaphor, will resort to the "flattened babble of E-mail."

It is clear from our previous discussions that there is a certain logic to the order or structure of liturgy. "Logic" here is not construed as "rational" or "reasonable," but in the literal sense as *Logos,* with a capital "L," namely, as the Word of God that in the interaction with the community shapes the order of the worship event. There is an inherent *logos* in the way in which the *Logos* seeks to become enfleshed in the community. The composer who transposes texts and the orchestrator who puts together the individual expressions and the people who will help enact them have the mandate to write the inherent *logos* of the Word into the score, the script, the bulletin, or whatever is prepared in advance to enable the worship event to take place. *Logos* as a rhetorical medium is integral to the shape of liturgy itself.

Likewise, *pathos* is a rhetorical element of liturgy that can be planned for as worship expressions are composed. The intent is not to program or manipulate people's emotional reactions but to allow the emotions that make us all human to be experienced in all their richness and fullness, even to give permission for those emotions to be expressed. Mainline Protestants in the latter half of the twentieth century reacted to the sentimentalities and emotionalisms that characterized the worship perspectives of their forbears a century earlier. We became wary, particularly with the advent of televangelists and their emotional contrivances, of anything that had any resemblance whatsoever to revival techniques and tent-meeting theatrics. However, as mainline denominations have begun to attract and cultivate more ethnically, racially, and culturally diverse congregations, these new communities, through hymnody and ritual, have given the traditional churches permission to explore the emotional dimensions of worship. Henry Mitchell says that "we have to become *intentional* about emotion in worship as a whole. . . . The powerful effects of emotion must begin to be systematically utilized, rather than merely tolerated."[28]

Scripture is full of *pathos* and rich with emotions. Transposing these texts involves allowing the inherent *pathos* in the texts themselves to become an element of the transposition. There is an amplitude of emotions ranging from laughter and "hallelujahs" to tears and lamentations throughout the worship event. Without allowing the *pathos* in the texts to become recontextualized, liturgy will become prosaic, and the brain waves of the worshipers will flatten out. Perhaps, like in a piece of music, there can be liturgical dynamic markings scripted into the bulletin to give the congregation permission to be expressive.

I participated in the Easter Great Vigil in a large metropolitan church. The initial parts of the service were penitential and preparatory and without instrumental accompaniment. Finally, when the leader announced, "The Lord is risen!" there was a direction in the worship folder inviting the congregation to *shout,* "The Lord is risen indeed!" Immediately nearly a thousand voices thundered the Easter acclamation, all the lights were turned up to full brightness, the organist laid hands and arms on all the manuals and both feet across the pedals, and the choir rang handbells. The cacophony of sound and light proclaimed with no uncertainty that at that moment Easter was happening.

Obviously to put all of that together demanded an extraordinary orchestration long *before* the camera-ready edition of the bulletin for that service was sent off to the printer. The emotional level at that moment was off the meter, yet none of us felt manipulated. As musicianship involves not only reproducing the notes on a score but also allowing the *pathos* intended by the composer to come to full expression, likewise in liturgy the goal of transposition is to allow the inherent *pathos* in the texts to meet the emotional life-texts of the community and thereby to offer a *sym-pathos* (literally a "like-feeling") through which the emotions each person brings to the worship gathering will be given permission to be expressed.

Crafting liturgy is different from writing a term paper. Unfortunately, the words I sometimes see printed in church bulletins, and even in denominational liturgical resources, are basically theological statements. The words of liturgy, however, are not meant to be descriptions *about* God, but words that invite the community to talk *with* God. Therefore, the human words that are crafted to become liturgical vessels of proclamation intentionally need to reflect homiletically and liturgically the *pathos* intrinsic to the Scriptures themselves and, in Henry Mitchell's words, by "the logic of emotive consciousness"[29] to invite people into the encounter with God. In this way the worshipers' emotions will not be manipulated by what the leader wants them to experience; the after-the-service response will be, "Pastor, that _____ (prayer, hymn, sermon, anthem, scripture lesson) was meant for me."

Robin Meyers, continuing from a homiletical perspective the contemporary work by Mary John Smith and others in rhetorical theory, classifies such an identification between speaker and listener as "self-persuasion" and proposes that sermons be crafted as *"intentional acts of self-persuasion."*[30] I maintain that the same can be said of crafting liturgy. The following penitential act to accompany the Gospel lesson in Luke 5:1–11, appointed for Epiphany 5 in Year C of the *Revised Common Lectionary,* hopefully is illustrative. Here the familiar Lukan version of Jesus' calling the disciples was transposed with an eye to metaphors shaped by the text that would offer an expression of *sym-pathos* in an assembly of pastors. The service began with the reading of one verse of the lection: "Jesus said to Simon, 'Put out into the deep water and let down your nets for a catch'" (Luke 5:4), followed by the hymn, "Jesus calls us" set to the tune RESTORATION. Then the penitential act began:

Leader: Simon answered, "Master, we have worked all night long
            but have caught nothing."   (Luke 5:5a)

All: *in unison*

            Lord Jesus, we come to you weary from our well-doing.
                We have worked day and night at ministry,
                    yet the fruits of our labors seem increasingly more marginal.
                Each idol in the vain world's golden store cries "worship me more!"
                    and ensnares us and our people into one more consuming pastime.
            O Jesus, how tired our bodies and souls are,
                and how empty our nets seem!
            Yet we have visions of big catches and boats brimming,
                and we dream wonderful dreams of being amazed
                by what a secularity says is unpredictable and unexpected.
            Show us, O Christ, a sign
                that all we have done for you has not been in vain,
                and convince us that our calling
                    is more than an echo of our own desire.
            At your word we will let down our nets again!

                                    silence

Leader: When they had done this, they caught so many fish
            that their nets were beginning to break....
            For all were amazed at the catch of fish that they had taken.   (Luke 5:6, 9)

Aristotle placed *ethos* first among the rhetorical disciplines because he
believed that the art of persuasion involved fundamentally the ethical character of the speaker. Again, a consideration of *ethos* is appropriate for the
discussion of *doing* liturgy that is the subject of chapter 6. Yet again, I raise
the issue here because the way leaders will lead liturgy in the assembly is
determined by the way in which the expressions are crafted before the
final manuscript for liturgy is printed and reproduced.

Ethos classically had to do with the perceived ethical character of the
speaker: Can this person be believed? We all have been in the presence
of persons, publicly and privately, who by the very way they present
themselves raise in others impressions that question their credibility and
sincerity. Obviously such a dimension of *ethos* is important to preaching
and liturgy. It was a negative *ethos* or a lack of *ethos* that brought down
several former bright stars in TV evangelism's heaven and in the process
lowered the public's perception of all clergy. My concern here is that since,
as stated earlier, leadership is part of liturgy itself, then the presence or

affect the worship leaders project has a significant role in the persuasive power of the liturgy not only in how it will be perceived by the worshiping community but also in how it will draw the community into the engagement with the Word of God. If the worship leaders draw attention to themselves, then the congregation can say, "What a wonderful preacher we have," or, negatively, as one person complained of her pastor, "I'm not going to _____ church anymore because the pastor makes funny faces during the sermon."

Interestingly the complaint about the pastor's "funny faces" reveals at a greater depth the power of the *persona* of the worship leader. *Persona* is the Latin word for the mask that the actor in Greek and Roman theater wore to portray a certain character. One actor could portray several characters by putting on different masks, or *personae*. What *personae* worship leaders will wear in next Sunday's worship is a decision that must be made long before next Sunday. These are not Halloween masks meant to disguise the wearers but personal faces through whom the community will see God. They are not "false faces," as we call the masks that are part of Halloween costumery, but the homiletical and liturgical faces that the Gospel fashions for the community's encounter with the reality of the Word of God. They are the "real" persons, the ones who will be part of the liturgy itself, through whom the congregation liturgically and homiletically will see God.

It is customary in some areas of Scotland for the request of the Greeks to Philip in John 12:21 to be carved into pulpits so that the words are visible only to the preacher: "Sir, we wish to see Jesus." "Seeing," in John's metaphoric language, obviously was not intended to refer to the eyes. Transposed to carvings on a pulpit, "we wish to see" becomes a request for a homiletical and liturgical encounter with Christ. Until my metaphor was changed by Paul Wilson, I said for years that the function of liturgical leadership is to become *transparent* so that the seekers would see only Jesus. Wilson's correction is so eloquent:

> God never intended the Word to be handled with sterile gloves, kept free from contact with anything human. If this had been the intention, Christ would not have come among us in human form. We may hope to be *translucent* [emphasis added], allowing God's light to shine through our words and actions. But we can never be transparent, as though we do not speak from our humanity. God alone

makes perfect the communication of the Word, in the heart and soul of the willing hearer. In this process God uses who we are in all our humanity to bear the Word.[31]

We cannot wait until Sunday morning's call to worship to compose and then orchestrate what needs to be done to allow translucence to happen in the worship service. For it to happen in the doing of liturgy it needs to be crafted *into* the liturgy. Translucence is a characteristic of the liturgy itself and can happen only through prayer and engagement with the Scriptures, through careful transpositions of the words and actions that will become parts of the liturgical experiences long before the leaders enter chancel and pulpit. Allowing the roles the *personae* will play in the liturgical enactment to arise out of the Scriptures and their liturgical transpositions will avoid attention being drawn to the leader's *personalities* that can block translucence and get in the way of the community's seeing "the light of the glory of God in the face of Jesus Christ" (2 Cor. 4:6). Therefore *ethos* in the true classical sense is the response the leaders cause, and it is "the listener who finally evaluates and thus individually determines the preacher's ethos."[32]

Meyers says that "preaching as self-persuasion regards the listener as the dominant partner in the persuasion process, the listeners must participate in the sermon before it is written."[33] Many years ago I began to craft sermons and liturgies with the eye of my imagination focused on particular persons who were regular worshipers in the congregations I served. I now have expanded the imaginary assembly to include specific pastors who regularly participate in our monthly services of Word and Sacrament for clergy. As I compose liturgy on my word processor, I "see" these persons in my mind and ask myself, "How will _____ hear this?" I do not mean, "Will he or she agree with what I am saying?" but, "How will these words that I am writing be heard given the life-texts that I know these persons will bring to the gathering?" This methodology is valid not only in the crafting of sermons but also in transposing the individual worship expressions and crafting the whole of the liturgy.

Overhearing the Familiar

Wordsworth and Coleridge, in the preface to the 1802 edition of the *Lyrical Ballads,* defined the role of poetry as making the familiar strange and the strange familiar. In crafting liturgy the role of worship leaders is to transpose a text that is familiar in one form into a new genre that allows worshipers to overhear the familiar in a new and refreshing way, like an old gemstone that in a new setting begins to sparkle with an attracting freshness. The idea of "overhearing the Gospel" in preaching was proposed by Fred Craddock more than thirty years ago out of his concern for listeners "who through old habits have already agreed in advance of hearing and therefore do not hear."[34] The task for preachers, he says, is "to enable hearers to walk down the corridors of their own minds, seeing anew old images hanging there, images that have served more powerfully than all concepts and generalization in shaping them into feeling, thinking, acting beings they are; to pronounce the old vocabulary so that someone hears a new cadence in it."[35]

Certainly the task is not restricted merely to the preaching of sermons. Many worshipers have agreed in advance to suspend spiritual involvement and maybe even their physical presence in some worship expressions and even whole services that they have predetermined will be a rerun of a less-than-fulfilling liturgical exercise. My father worshiped regularly in the congregation in which he served as a lay elder, and regularly he also complained to me — and perhaps to the pastor also — about the liturgy, "Page three, every week page three." The liturgy that began on page three was and still is a liturgical classic, yet the mechanical manner in which it was enacted invited a boredom that, in Craddock's words, "works against the faith by provoking contrary thoughts or lulling to sleep or draping the whole occasion with a pall of indifference and unimportance."[36]

There are those who claim that the church in an electronic age when boredom easily sets in must scrap the page-threes and provide "alternative" or "contemporary" worship experiences if churches are to grow into megachurches.[37] Those of us who are old enough to remember find such dictums not-so-new at all. The music may have gotten louder and the TV screens bigger through the development of more sophisticated electronics, the drum accompaniments more ubiquitous and praise chorus more repetitious, yet the underlying assumptions are the same: Give people what an electronic consumer culture has convinced them they think they need and want. However, Marva Dawn asks, "If television is causing people to be dissatisfied with the worship of our churches, should we change worship to be more like television — or should the splendor of our worship cause people to ask better questions about television?"[38] She comments,

Music, songs, Scripture lessons, sermons, liturgical forms, architecture, and other accouterments of art and gesture and ambience are all means by which God invites, reveals, and forms us. If we use shallow (I did not say *simple*) worship materials, they will not reveal the truth about God. Instead these shallow materials will shape shallow theology and form us superficially.[39]

Fred Craddock's warnings to an earlier generation tempted by the same forces perhaps are even more poignant today: "resist the idea of being peddlers, willing to brighten the drab occasion and chase away monotony with sideshows and bargains."[40] Liturgical expressions that arise organically out of the scripture texts will help to immerse people into the wonder of God's splendor because that's what the Bible story is about. Worship events shaped by the form of God's own self-revelation instead of continually pandering to people's perception of their religious needs and focusing on the bad or good experiences of the human condition will offer an inviting alternative to the hype the culture turns up to sell its meaninglessness. Worship is a counter-cultural event, and, when its focus is on God, worship becomes very attractive simply because God attracts! People tired of the culture's reruns will begin to overhear — perhaps even for the first time — the old, old story that seeks again to awaken those dozing in boredom and to revitalize the body that is Christ's in today's world.

Every Christmas pageant includes bathrobed shepherds (generally boys) saying monotonously in less-than-a-unison response to the angels, "Let us go now to Bethlehem and see this thing that has taken place, which the Lord has made known to us" (Luke 2:15b). Suppose this familiar text is transposed into a call to worship, at the very beginning of the service, inviting the community — plus some one-time-a-year visitors — into the Christ-mass:

Leader: Let us go now to Bethlehem and see this thing that has taken place, which
         the Lord has made known to us.   (Luke 2:15b)

The congregation may stand.

All: *singing*   GLORIA

         Angels we have heard on high, sweetly singing o'er the plains.
         And the mountains in reply, echoing their joyous strains.
         Gloria in excelsis Deo! Gloria in excelsis Deo!

Solo: Shepherds, why this jubilee? Why your joyous strains prolong?
             What the gladsome tidings be which inspire your heavenly song?

All: **Gloria in excelsis Deo! Gloria in excelsis Deo!**

All: **Come to Bethlehem and see Him whose birth the angels sing;**
            Come, adore on bended knee Christ, the Lord, the newborn King.
            Gloria in excelsis Deo! Gloria in excelsis Deo!

Note the sense of motion that occurs when text and hymn are juxtaposed with each other. The familiar Scripture in a new context invites the worshipers' participation in the event and suggests a movement, if not of the body itself, at least of the mind and heart, into a new place, an alternative place, where God is doing a new thing. As the leader invites, *"Let us go and see . . . ,"* people are drawn through their imagination into the journey to Bethlehem, the place of Bread, where they will be nourished in Word and Sacrament. The interrogatory hymn stanza, suggested here as sung by a soloist, gives voice to the seeker's question, the human uncertainty, of what will be happening in this event. The soloist may walk searchingly while singing the stanza as if trying somehow to follow a procession without knowing whence it came and what its destination is. Finally, in the third stanza the community, now liturgically in the sacred space of Bethlehem, invite themselves — and the onlookers and passersby: *"Come* to Bethlehem and see . . . ," *"Come,* adore. . . . "

Bethlehem's place has come to their worship space as it will on countless Christmas Eves and in innumerable settings. The Scripture itself — a very familiar verse — has suggested a musical accompaniment to its overhearing and has shaped a new liturgical journey. The text has been enacted in a very simple and uncomplicated way that doesn't need professional musicians to be effective, yet hopefully the transposition becomes a mode of being touched by God's Word in a new, that is, Gospel, way. By the way, the initial call, "Come, let us go to Bethlehem . . . " still can and maybe should be spoken by children, but without bathrobes, please! The transposition invites the community to go not to the Bethlehem of antiquity but to the place of the new nativity.

Another way of enabling the congregation to overhear the familiar is to set well-known hymns to new tunes, maybe not new in themselves inasmuch as the congregation may be accustomed to singing the "new" tune to a different hymn text, but "new" to that particular set of words. The juxtaposition of the familiar words with a tune that may be "strange" invites the worshipers to experience a new dimension of a text that some even may have committed to memory. Charles Wesley's beloved hymn "Love Divine, All Loves Excelling" generally on the American scene is set to the march-like tune BEECHER, composed by John Zundel and named after Henry Ward Beecher, minister of Plymouth Congregational Church in Brooklyn, New York, where Zundel was the organist for many years. In the memory bank of most veteran American churchgoers this text is wedded to this tune. British congregations, however, are accustomed to singing Wesley's hymn to HYFRYDOL by the Welsh composer Rowland Hugh Prichard. HYFRYDOL in American hymnals is linked with a number of texts, yet none of them have the same identification as "Love Divine" with BEECHER. Some more recent hymnbooks published in the United States set "Love Divine" to HYFRYDOL or suggest it as an alternate to BEECHER. Interestingly, *hyfrydol* means "pleasant" and "melodious" in Welsh, and congregations may discover that this tune named after such a lovely Welsh word is perhaps a more appropriate accompaniment to words that speak of God's love that excels all other human loves.

The juxtaposition of a "strange" tune with a familiar text may become a mode of inviting the worshipers into an experience of the Gospel, particularly on Transfiguration Sunday (Last after Epiphany). Wesley's words that end in "... lost in wonder, love, and praise" then become a descant to the evangelists' accounts on the mountain when God's Word was transfigured to human eyes and to the Torah's narrative (in Years A and C) of Moses' experience of God's presence on Mt. Sinai (Exod. 24:12–18 and 34:29–35).

In transposing texts into worship expressions the leader has the awesome responsibility of allowing the Good News of Jesus Christ to shape the form and content of the liturgical action and, at the same time, to avoid novelties that draw attention to the leader's own personality or become devices the leader or planner uses to manipulate people. Paul Wilson says so eloquently:

> Many of the words we commonly use to talk about the faith have lost their spark. Repeated use of them without exposing them to imagination will have no more positive effect on the congregation than will raising the voice in giving directions to someone who does not speak our language.... The solution is not just to cut back on the use of these words.... Nor is the solution to eliminate them

entirely. . . . *The words of the Christian faith are gifts to us. They are trea-sures of which we are the stewards: We cannot let them die, for they can be the route to true life.* . . . The solution has to do with language renewal. Just as words can decay and die, so too can they be renewed and have fresh life. The words of our faith are precious, yet they sometimes litter the floor like unthreshed husks of wheat. Some people would tread on them underfoot. . . . When these same words are gathered up with care and thrown into the air, the Holy Spirit has a chance to blow through them, to winnow them, to sift out the good news anew. They are renewed when they are seen or heard as though for the first time, when they have life again, when people want to use them because they have again become important for them.[41]

Newness that participates in the Gospel has its origin in the Word of God that seeks to be heard always anew. The church has the responsibility in each generation of making what has been handed on in Scripture and tra-dition its own. However, liturgical novelties that leaders and communities, with benign and sometimes evangelical intent, seek to utilize to relate to people's needs, desires, and experiences frequently end up as mere con-trivances that do not lead people to God. Calvin said that those "who introduce newly invented methods of worshiping God really worship and adore the creature of their own distempered imaginations."[42]

I recently attended a worship service of a large gathering of people from throughout the United States. All the hymns chosen were unfamiliar to most of the assembly. These hymns had integrity in themselves and reflected a diversity of cultural and racial worship traditions. Yet most of those gathered on this occasion, including those with considerable musical skills, could not sing all those new texts and tunes and rhythms on the spot. I am sure that the purpose of including these particular hymns was to expose a large national gathering of the church to some wonderful new worship expressions. However, without preparation the congregation could not assimilate so many newnesses at one time, and, rather than enabling the assembly to participate in the newness of the Gospel, these "strange" hymns resulted in an almost angry disengagement of many from the worship service.

In crafting liturgies I seek to ensure that the tune, if not also the words, of the first hymn or musical expression always will be a familiar one. Some church musicians believe that a congregation can assimilate no more than four to six new hymn tunes a year. Such a dictum seems terribly restrictive to those who would want to bring about rapid liturgical renewal, yet newness without a genuine appropriation of the Good News that the expression seeks to proclaim simply ends up being novelty for novelty's sake. Hymns, like all other worship expressions, are not ends in themselves but aim to be vessels to allow the divine-human dialogue to take place. To enable overhearing by wedding a new text with a familiar tune or by interchanging familiar texts and tunes is a less radical approach that may open the community to hearing and responding in a way that builds up the body of Christ in love.

Connecting with the Community

My discussions, although hopefully amplified with illustrative liturgical transpositions, have been primarily conceptual. But before we turn to the next chapter and immerse ourselves in the process that shapes the liturgical action, we need to face the bottom-line question: Do the *worshipers* perceive these transpositions as connected to the biblical texts? And, as such, do these transpositions help people to be engaged by the Word of God in the worship event? While I was active in parish ministry I conducted another study that was aimed at surveying to what extent people were able to perceive the transposition of biblical texts into liturgical acts. On two successive Sundays worshipers were asked to register what they felt was the correlation between the text(s) appointed in the *Revised Common Lectionary* and the worship expressions I either authored myself or chose from other sources as liturgical transpositions of those texts. As in the earlier study I placed brackets in the bulletins next to the headings of those acts for which I was asking them to register their perceptions. If people were to be asked to register the correlation between biblical text(s) and worship acts, especially those that would take place prior to the public reading of the text(s), I printed excerpts or verses of the texts in the opening instructions in the worship bulletins. Also those who introduced the texts would give worshipers a few moments to read the excerpts or point them out in the liturgy before the worship began.

In the task of crafting these liturgies, the staff of the church and I were quite intentional in transposing texts into different genres and in preserving a sense of organic unity among the worship expressions. I could not deliberately create, for example, a prayer of confession that would have been the transposition of a totally unrelated biblical text simply as a device to test whether or not people could perceive a correlation. Nor could I choose a hymn generally associated with an Easter text for the first Sunday of Advent merely to try to find out whether people might indicate that it didn't correspond to the lectionary text(s) for Christ the King Sunday. What a worship leader is called to handle is too sacred a trust to be profaned by self-motivated experiments. And what is most sacred are not the biblical texts themselves, nor the liturgical expressions that tradition has hallowed, nor the physical worship space, but the *worshipers'* corporate experience of God's speaking and acting through these expressions.

Although it is difficult in any study involving an exercise as subjective as worship to sort out people's hermeneutical ability from their tastes, the responses revealed that people could perceive the transpositions of biblical texts and that they discerned a high degree of correlation between the texts and the various worship expressions, including the hymns and other musical offerings. In fact, a few responses indicated that these persons perceived a higher degree of correlation in the musical parts of the service than in the sermon! What a shock to one's homiletical ego!

Were these results, again, an isolated phenomenon or would worshipers in other congregations be able to perceive the transpositions as well as this congregation did? As Conference Minister I asked five pastors to conduct the same surveys that I had used. Again the results were almost identical to what I discovered in another congregation seventeen hundred miles away. Most of the responses showed a correlation between the texts and the transpositions. Interestingly, although all five pastors conducted the surveys on the same Sundays with the same lectionary texts, their transpositions were as varied as the worship styles of the churches they serve. In a church served by one of the pastors the worship tradition is the prayer-book style in which the liturgical texts for each Sunday's service are read corporately from the texts printed in the front of the hymnals. On the other hand, in a church served by another pastor, the style is far more of the free-church variety with most of the corporate worship expressions printed in the bulletin. Yet what was striking among the variety of worship styles and differences in transpositions was that worshipers saw direct correlations between the texts and the worship expressions peculiar to each congregation. In assessing why all pastors had found very similar survey results one concluded: "Since the *experience* of worship is not a cognitive event, we all came out with the same results."

Regarding what this group of pastors learned from the exercise, one commented, "A majority [of worshipers] felt a sense of approval that the service has a unity of scriptural themes. Even the anthems carried the theme. The junior choir director became aware [through the survey] that the anthem also fits with the scriptural theme." Another pastor said, "I now print a text for the whole worship service at the top of the bulletin." Still another said that he learned that the concept of a liturgy based on the lectionary text(s) is a way of attacking "the problem of biblical illiteracy." "When a text is transposed into a particular act," he went on, "this is an act of interpretation and application of the text to a different aspect of life." The exercise, one pastor said, "taught me the importance of crafting the whole liturgy." Another pastor realized after conducting the surveys that he was "enlightened as to how much people notice what's going on in worship. They are more aware than I gave them credit for." One pastor realized that her work as worship leader was now expanded: "The variety of forms in the services was very helpful. It inspired me to venture forth creatively on my own. The only downside: It now takes me about three more hours each week to prepare the service!" Yes, now that you've put it all together and can venture out on your own, it *will* take you longer to get ready for Sunday!

FIVE

Orchestrating Worship

Getting ready for Sunday and putting it all together is what this chapter is all about. It is about orchestrating worship — about putting together, arranging, organizing the event so as to allow the appointed worship hour to be a time when the congregation can do its worship work and be open to God performing miraculously and wondrously with this gathered people of God. By the way, the verbs "put together," "arrange," and "organize" are lifted directly from my dictionary's definition of "orchestrate."

Generally we conceive of "orchestrate" in musical terms. As I am writing this chapter, I also am rehearsing along with 235 other singers for two performances of Leonard Bernstein's "Chichester Psalms" with a world-renowned orchestra and maestro. Although the chorus has rehearsed for months, it was only yesterday, in the first of two rehearsals, that the singers joined the other musicians of the orchestra. What happened at that moment when Bernstein's orchestration of these ancient and beloved Hebrew psalms came together became to some of us participants a truly liturgical and spiritual experience. Was this happening the result of Bernstein's transposition of the texts? Of the musical preparation of the orchestra and the singers? Of the maestro's conducting? All of the above contributed as they were put together for this musical event. And what made it for some of us a spiritual experience? The maestro standing there waving a thin stick at some 300 people? Who conducted [literally "led together"] this orchestration of vocal and instrumental sounds into what for some of us became a transcendent moment?

In some quarters "orchestrate" has become a tainted word and turned into a synonym for "manipulate." Most of us on occasion have been

manipulated by orchestrators who have turned worship into a performance by pulpiteer preachers and musical virtuosos. Choirs rearrange
themselves so as to "perform" a musical rendition more visibly and audi-
bly, and their performance is rewarded with applause. The accompaniment
is an electronic tape of a thirty-piece orchestra that never could fit inside
such a tiny building. The assembly becomes an audience, the chancel a
sound stage, the nave an auditorium, while the performers do their stage
act. The master of ceremonies in one such mega-gathering of which I
was part told the audience: "We don't want to offend anyone when we
take up an offering. So if you're new here, just sit back, relax, and enjoy
the music." I didn't. I didn't put anything in the plate, I didn't sit back
and relax, and I didn't enjoy the band's rendition of "When the Saints
Go Marching In." It was a celebration of the Fourth of July that was
orchestrated on that sound stage — with some very sophisticated electronic gadgets, by the way! In this chapter I hope to recover the rightful
and original meaning of this metaphor. "Orchestrating" here is about
homiletical-liturgical arranging, organizing, and putting together. (My pastor neighbor's question, "How do I put it all together?" is still being asked
throughout these conversations.)

Orchestral Leadership

To avoid a cacophony of liturgical discordance and to allow an organic
harmony to arise from the texts, the community mandates (from the Latin
mandare, to "hand over") to *someone* the responsibility to orchestrate worship. In the main I use the generic term "worship leader" to designate
the person mandated this responsibility. Although Paul said that he did
not receive the apostolic mandate by conferring "with any human being"
(Gal. 1:16b), the Christian community soon after the first generation of
such charismatic appointments found ways to designate those among the
baptized on whom the homiletical and liturgical mantle would fall. This
is not the place for an excursion into the rather complicated history of
the development of orders of ministry. Suffice it to say, Christian communities throughout history have called some of their own and entrusted
to them the awesome responsibility of orchestrating and leading liturgy.[1]
These are not the primary "do-ers" of liturgy. The community, as we shall
see in the next chapter, does liturgy. Leaders do the orchestrating, the
arranging, the organizing, the putting together so that the community

will have before them the texts and the transpositions of those texts that will enable them to be about their worship work and to invite God's Word to happen again in their midst.

Generally today the primary responsibility for orchestrating worship is entrusted to the church's pastors and priests. The final shaping that takes place during the immediate days preceding Sunday is in the hands of the one whom the community designates as its *klerikos,* or, in archaic English, its "clerk," the "literate person." He or she has the homiletical and liturgical skills "to write" the final edition of Sunday's sermon and liturgy on behalf of the community. By whatever method and tradition the task is handed over to the *klerikoi,* they are the ones generally who from week to week have this awesome opportunity to orchestrate the community's worship. Hopefully these leaders have been exposed to and understand the *orthodoxia* so that they are freed to transpose as the Word of God through the Scriptures seeks ways to be embodied in the life of the church. I shall simply assume that such training in *orthodoxia* has been part of the orchestrators' core academic preparation for ministry and that continual education will occur as the church remains willing to insist on learned-ness among its leaders.

As I make such an assumption, however, I know that some will stand before some congregations next Sunday ill prepared to touch and handle things unseen despite their eagerness to respond to the call of God. The gaps are glaring, even frightening. Yet I know that orchestrating worship is something that can be learned, and I have spent thirty-five years in workshops, classrooms, and retreats helping clergy and lay leaders catch the vision that putting it all together for worship is a wonderfully exciting and awesome adventure. Although such primary responsibility for orchestration is mandated to the one called as pastor and priest, his or her art is never practiced in solitary confinement. In the week before Sunday, even weeks and months before, other persons with varied spiritual gifts have been working, sometimes in separate workshops, to craft the components that will be orchestrated by the *klerikos.*

The roles of each of the leaders — including the pastor and priest — are mandated by the liturgy itself. Gordon Lathrop is so right in saying fundamentally that "the leadership of the liturgy is part of the liturgy."[2] Ordination grows out of the need for persons to be responsible for the *order* of the liturgy. *The leadership roles in worship are defined by the way in which the community will do liturgy*. Each ecclesiastical tradition has developed criteria for designating those who have roles in the enactment of liturgy. In some churches persons are ordained to specific functions in the liturgy — for example, in presbyterial polities the ordination of elders to assist in the distribution of the communion elements. There are some ecclesiastical traditions that even today ban all musical instruments from worship and rely solely on the singing of the community as the musical accompaniment to liturgy.

One could argue that such decisions are made on the basis of issues that are not inherent in the doing of liturgy itself. Will there be lectors to read the scripture passages, liturgists to assist in the leading of liturgical expressions, cantors to chant or sing portions of the psalms, ushers to receive the community's gifts? The list of leaders is an ever-expanding one, especially as congregations seek to allow a diversity of gifts to come to expression. Yet it is the liturgy itself that shapes the leadership of the liturgy. Worship leaders are not appointed simply to give somebody "something to do" to keep him or her involved in the life of the community. Liturgy itself will involve all the community — including children — and will define the roles of worship leaders — including children. Worship in the shape of Scripture will shape the worship leaders who will, in turn, enable the community to do the work of liturgy in worshiping God.

Those who have been gifted with certain talents and have practiced their art can be invited to offer their contributions to the enactment of worship as a stewarding of God's abundance intended to be given back to God in the worship of God. The role of worship leaders is not to perform but to offer, and the difference between the two is basically a faith issue. Performance as an end in itself either for personal fulfillment or for monetary reward is fostered in our culture by the entertainment industry, particularly through electronic media. Performers draw attention to themselves and make big bucks for themselves. Offering in worship is a counter-cultural endeavor in which leaders *give away* attention and talents to God in gratitude and obedience. The human experience in the act of offering is not a reward of self-gratification for one's gift, which nonprofit organizations are particularly adept at cultivating in donors (especially in response to large donations), but is discerning an at-one-ness with that which is beyond the self, outside the self, a being filled with that which is more than bread. Those charged with orchestrating worship have the almost impossible mission of helping worship leaders catch an alternative vision of how they employ their gifts in worship. A choir, for example, who come to see their role as an offering of their combined vocal gifts to God become instruments through whom God effects the Word of God. Their gift of their transposition of the Scriptures is therefore integral to the doing of liturgy, and they themselves thereby become part of the liturgy.

The age-old question about what music is appropriate for worship has been addressed from a variety of perspectives ranging from the strict Calvinist interpretation that only the words of Scripture set to music for the community's singing are allowed to an almost "anything goes" subjectivism that whatever produces a mood within the individual worshiper is acceptable. Carol Doran (a musician) and Thomas Troeger (a homiletician/liturgiologist) have worked together for years to help worship leaders understand that music and preaching are integrally related disciplines. In a jointly produced volume they say,

> To contrast the ministry of the Word of God and the ministry of music represents a human dichotomy of what in truth is one divine reality. We hear the Word of God spoken in the sermon, but that same Word many come to us in another form through the music.[3]

A very perceptive minister of music once said to me, "Russ, if you think everyone is with you at every point throughout the service, you're kidding yourself." The studies referenced earlier that other pastors and I conducted in a variety of settings corroborate what she and the Doran-Troeger team have said. Different people are engaged with the Word of God through different liturgical expressions.

The underlying premise to the conversations in this volume is that the crafting of liturgy, and therefore any musical or other artistic accompaniment, involves an act of interpretation in which the texts of Scripture seek to be transposed into liturgical expressions. That is, the role of worship leaders as interpreters for the community is to allow the texts to do in their new liturgical context in the community what they do in their settings in the Bible. Therefore, the texts themselves become the focus of any liturgical shaping, and the primary hermeneutical question becomes: "Will this transposition of a scripture text — verbal or nonverbal, musical or graphic — be a vessel through which this particular community may be engaged by the Word of God?" And the second question is: "Will this particular transposition work organically with other expressions in this particular order of worship as one part of an integrated whole so that there can be a *communal* experience of the Word of God?"

Orchestration of worship therefore involves working collegially with all the leaders who will be part of any given worship service. Putting together what will become the various components of liturgy includes engaging well in advance the lectionary texts with musicians, educators, storytellers, technical assistants, and even with those who will be arranging the physical space in which the worship will take place to insure that all are working on the same score and that, come Sunday, organic liturgy will happen. Such reading together of the texts and sketching in broad strokes the shape each service may take can occur on a quarterly or even semiannual basis. Each leader then can work in his or her own discipline with the others who will be invited to offer their gifts. The orchestrator is one of a team of interpreters and becomes the enabler to assist the whole team in their individual engagements with the texts.

Hymns are not to provide some stage-setting music for the sermon, and therefore their selection is not the prerogative of the preacher. The hymns themselves are part of the whole community's conversation with the text, and so the orchestrator has the responsibility to be in creative dialogue with those responsible for the musical interpretations and transpositions. Worship planning in staff meetings can become exciting opportunities for corporate Bible study and liturgical education. In my final years as a parish pastor I had the privilege of working collegially with a wonderfully gifted minister of music who was both well-schooled in *orthodoxia* yet very creative in transposing texts musically. We met with the other staff persons responsible for various aspects of the life of that congregation, outlined the major festivals and events, and engaged the appointed Scriptures in semiannual mini-retreats. Each of us continued in our own ways to live with the texts, preparing those expressions that were indigenous to each of our ministries. When it came time to begin putting together what would become the liturgy for each particular worship service, the minister of music and I *together* selected the hymns and other liturgical expressions that in our estimation would become the best transpositions of the texts for that community. Sometimes this work consumed several hours, yet I continue to affirm that in the years we worked together every hymn that was sung in that congregation was selected mutually.

However, in the latter days prior to Sunday the finishing that puts everything together resides with that one person whom the community has called and entrusted with this homiletical and liturgical responsibility. The final worship orchestration cannot be done in committee nor by the church secretary opening up a bulletin mock-up file into which next Sunday's specials are inserted. The leader goes to his or her own solitary workshop — nowadays most often a computer station like mine in an upper room — orchestrates what others have transposed in their settings, what tradition has handed on that has the potential of sparkling afresh in this forthcoming setting, what the community's texts of trial and rejoicing have been recording, and what has been arising out of the orchestrator's own living with the texts of Scripture. It is time for the leader to put it all together.

Scoring the Flow

As the liturgy is being shaped on the computer monitor, I scroll back and forth with an "eye" to the flow of the various expressions within the liturgical structure, and in my imagination I try to "see" the liturgy being enacted in the particular setting in which that particular assembly will gather. I check to ensure that no two musical expressions are placed back-to-back. Very few keyboard musicians are trained in the art of modulation from one key and rhythm to another. Starting to play a second piece of music abruptly immediately after the conclusion of the first causes a disjuncture in the liturgical flow. This is particularly noticeable when stanzas of different Christmas carols are linked together. Placing a spoken expression between two musical ones not only heightens a sense of the dialogical but also provides for the natural progression of the liturgical action to take place.

Liturgy has a beginning and an end, and between the first sound of the gathering to the final reverberation of the dismissal the liturgical expressions lead organically from one to another as the structure of the divine-human interaction unfolds. There is an innate rhythm that pulses throughout the liturgical action and keeps it moving toward its final resolution as a series of musical chords leads to a discernable resolution of the progression. Newman is correct in his assessment that often "theological treatments of worship have customarily thought of worship more in terms of order or structure than in terms of movement. . . . Modern study of the nature of language and symbol . . . has provided a conceptual basis for thinking of worship in relational and dynamic rather than in static terms."[4] In some African American assemblies it is the role of the keyboardist and drummer(s) to maintain the beat of the liturgy. Orchestration involves scoring the rests and repeats, that is, to decide where the appropriate times for corporate silence are and to determine what particular expressions deserve repetition, as illustrated in the sample score on page 111. Orchestration involves envisioning the inherent *flow* from one expression to the next *before* the words and expressions are put together in whatever form is ultimately necessary for the leaders and the congregation to do liturgy. The critical question for the leader in the drafting stage is: Does this liturgy seem to *move* organically from beginning to end as the texts are transposed and the expressions link themselves together in a liturgical progression?

Scoring the Splendor

Obviously the Easter acclamation wants to be shouted. Yet there also are occasions in every worship service for planned, purposeful silence. People need moments of stopping in liturgy for personal reflection, and there also are times of corporate silences when the orchestrated rest — as conceived musically — itself becomes a proclamatory event inviting God to break the silence with the Word. Orchestrating the rests is part of the art of liturgical crafting. To decide how much silence there shall be and when it shall occur in the flow of liturgy engages the same processes involved in transposing texts. The silent expressions (that's not an oxymoron!) sometimes will arise from the texts themselves. Generally I find that orchestrated silence in most worship services is either nonexistent, the result of poor timing (of which we shall speak more in the next chapter), or is too brief. Somehow Protestants have gotten the notion that silence is dangerous to one's health, and many people become uneasy if the duration of silence exceeds ten seconds. There is a great need for liturgical education around the role of silence in worship and in everyday life.

The old argument of the 1960s and 1970s regarding "traditional" and "contemporary" worship has recycled itself particularly in relation to the church-growth movement. Another flavor named "blended" has been added to the menu of options. As the liturgical wars are waged, "traditional" generally has come to be exemplified by the lofty words and music of nineteenth-century British "high-church" liturgists and musicians that call for proper enactment with pipe organ and well-trained choir. The style is contemplative. "Contemporary" in the 1960s mode meant folk songs accompanied by acoustic guitar. The style was folksy and intimate. Today "contemporary" is a synonym for songs — often sung by solo voices amplified — that are rhythmic, musically and lyrically repetitious, and accompanied as least minimally by electronic keyboards and drums. The mode is entertainment, the volume generally is loud, and the performers are rewarded with the audience's applause. "Blended" has come to mean some of all of the above. Unfortunately the wars sometimes have maneuvered the various camps into exclusive and absolutist positions and correctness.

I have come to learn that "contemporary" is not a prerequisite for church growth. I have witnessed growing churches whose style of worship would be labeled "traditional" by some. I also have observed some dying churches struggling to keep afloat by employing musical leadership committed to "contemporary" worship styles. And I can count both growing and dying congregations that have attempted "blended" worship. Sometimes, I believe, the rejection of what is perceived of as "traditional" is really a rejection of the unimaginative and downright boring ways in which some expressions, particularly musical ones, are executed in many assemblies. I agree with Marva Dawn that "style is not the issue. What matters is that whatever songs or forms we use keep us aware that God has invited us into worship, that God is present, that God is eminently worthy to receive our praise.... The question is whether our worship services immerse us in God's splendor."[5]

From this perspective, then, the labels become irrelevant, and, "we will stop fighting over the wrong questions, the marketers' opinions, cultural pressures, unbiblical solutions."[6] Those responsible for orchestrating liturgy will discover that there are innumerable expressions through which the Scriptures can recontextualize themselves — some as old as the Bible itself, some as new as what emerges from the orchestrator's own imagination; some comfortably familiar and others begging to be listened to for the first time; some contemplative and introspective, others pulsing with the rhythms and languages of cultures quite different from the community's common practice — all accompanied by voices singing and speaking, by instruments both electronic and acoustical, by clapping and dance, by architecture and visual arts. God's gifts to people are many-splendored, and when many talents and tongues are orchestrated well, the community experiences being immersed liturgically in the full orchestra of God's own splendor. Authentic worship is both traditional and contemporary simultaneously; worship leaders have the wonderful opportunity, as no other vocation is mandated, to bring together the people and to put together the expressions that lead to this awesome immersion into the very being of God.

Finishing the Score

Orchestration involves putting everything together and creating a liturgical score that will enable the congregation to do their worship work. The score may or may not appear in printed form. It may or may not all be written out. Nevertheless, there needs to be a script or score for the worship leaders to know what comes next. If the congregation is to do more than say "Amen" and sing a few hymns either by memory or from a hymnal, they also will need a score. I will discuss what generally is called a "bulletin" in the next chapter, but what I am about here is the final scoring that may or may not lead to a bulletin but must be part of the ahead-of-time orchestration of the worship event.

Scoring during the week hopefully ensures that everything on Sunday will come together. On the following pages is a score for a worship service based upon the lections for All Saints Day/Sunday in Year B. The *Revised Common Lectionary* directs that the texts for All Saints Day also may be used on the first Sunday in November. Some of the individual expressions are the same samples I shared in the previous chapter. In this score all are orchestrated together with additional hymns, prayers, musical responses, and complementary scripture texts for a common worship experience. What appears here is essentially a reproduction of the bulletin for a worship service for pastors. However, since doing ministry is not restricted to those with certain degrees and ecclesiastic endorsements, the service may be appropriate for any assembly celebrating the ministry of all the saints. The melody lines are printed in the body of the text as they would be in a bulletin. The keyboard accompaniments may be found on pages 165–167.

Service of Word and Sacrament
for
All Saints Day/Sunday

GATHERING

PROCESSIONAL   *The assembly may stand.*

CALL TO WORSHIP — Revelation 21:3b–4

HYMN   SINE NOMINE

For all the saints who from their labors rest,
who to the world their steadfast faith confessed,
Your name, O Jesus, be forever blessed.   Alleluia! Alleluia!

You were their rock, their refuge and their might;
You, Lord, their captain in the well-fought fight;
You, in the darkness drear, their one true light.   Alleluia! Alleluia!

Ringed by this cloud of witnesses divine,
We feebly struggle, they in glory shine;
Yet in your love our faithful lives entwine.   Alleluia! Alleluia!

Words: William Walsham How, 1864, alt.

PENITENCE

Leader: Since we are surrounded by so great a cloud of witnesses,
           Let us lay aside every weight and the sin that clings so closely,

All: And let us run with perseverance the race that is set before us,
           looking to Jesus the pioneer and perfecter of our faith.

(Heb. 12:1–2a)

Please be seated.

Leader: Let us pray:

All: O God of Martha and Lazarus and of all the saints
               who have proclaimed that Jesus Christ is Lord,
               we come to you in the poverty of our own profession.
           There have been those opportunities to minister that we have avoided
               and occasions to bring healing that we have passed by.

In the tombs of our own vulnerabilities we stay bound to the past
and chained to the routines we find most comfortable.
The remembrances of "if only I had been there" haunt us to tears
and mark with pain the sins of whatever we have left undone.

Lord, have mercy on us.   *silence*

Christ, have mercy on us.   *silence*

Lord, have mercy on us.   *silence*

Leader: Be assured that the grace of God overflows for us
with the faith and love that are in Christ Jesus.
The saying is sure and worthy of full acceptance,
that Christ Jesus came into the world to save sinners.

(1 Tim. 1:14–15, adapt.)

Sisters and brothers, believe the good news:
In Jesus Christ we are forgiven!

All: **To the Sovereign of ages, immortal, invisible, the only God,**
be honor and glory forever and ever.   (1 Tim. 1:14–15, 17, adapt.)

Response:

Al - le - lu - ia,   Al - le - lu - ia!

Music by Ralph Vaughan Williams (1872–1958) from *The English Hymnal* by permission of
Oxford University Press.

WORD

PSALM 24:

Reader 1: The earth is the Lord's and the fullness thereof,

Reader 2: the world, and those who dwell therein;

All: **For God has founded it on the seas,**
and established it on the rivers.

Response: (*singing*) **Alleluia! Alleluia!**

Reader 1: Who shall ascend the hill of the Lord?

Reader 2: and who shall stand in God's holy place?

All: **Those who have clean hands and pure hearts,**
who do not lift up their souls to what is false,
and do not swear deceitfully.

Reader 1: They will receive blessing from the Lord,

Reader 2: and vindication from the God of their salvation.

All: **Such is the company of those who seek the Lord,**
who seek the face of the God of Jacob.

Response: (*singing*) **Alleluia! Alleluia!**

Reader 1: Lift up your heads, O gates! and be lifted up, O ancient doors!
that the Ruler of glory may come in.

Reader 2: Who is the Ruler of glory?

All: **The Sovereign, strong and mighty,**
the Sovereign, mighty in battle.

Reader 1: Lift up your heads, O gates! and be lifted up, O ancient doors!
that the Ruler of glory may come in.

Reader 2: Who is the Ruler of glory?

All: **The Sovereign of hosts is the Ruler of glory.**   (Ps. 24, adapt.)

Response: (*singing*) **Alleluia! Alleluia!**

Leader: Let those who have ears to hear
listen to what the Spirit is saying to the churches.

The assembly may stand.

GOSPEL LESSON: John 11:32–44

Leader: This is the Good News!

All: (*singing*) **Alleluia! Alleluia!**

Please be seated.

SERMON: Doing Ministry Where It Stinks

Jesus said, "Take away the stone." Martha, the sister of the dead man, said to him, "Lord, already there is a stench because he has been dead four days." . . . So they took away the stone. And Jesus . . . cried with a loud voice, "Lazarus, come out!" The dead man came out, his hands and feet bound with strips of cloth, and his face wrapped in a cloth. Jesus said to them, "Unbind him, and let him go."   (John 11:39–44)

Leader: Now to the One who by the power at work within us is able to accomplish
            abundantly far more than all we can ask or imagine,

All: **to God be glory in the church and in Christ Jesus to all generations,
            forever and ever.**   (Eph. 3:20–21)

Response: (*singing*) **Alleluia! Alleluia!**

AFFIRMATION OF FAITH:

Leader: With the whole church let us affirm the faith of our baptism.

                                The congregation may stand.

Leader: Do you believe in God?

All: **I believe in God, the Father almighty, creator of heaven and earth.**

Leader: Do you believe in Jesus Christ?

All: **I believe in Jesus Christ, God's only Son, our Lord,
                who was conceived by the Holy Spirit,
                born of the Virgin Mary,
                suffered under Pontius Pilate,
                was crucified, died, and was buried;
                he descended to the dead.
            On the third day he rose again;
                he ascended into heaven,
                he is seated at the right hand of the Father,
                and he will come to judge the living and the dead.**

Leader: Do you believe in the Holy Spirit?

All: **I believe in the Holy Spirit,
                the holy catholic church,
                the communion of saints,
                the forgiveness of sins,
                the resurrection of the body,
            and the life everlasting. Amen.**

                                Please be seated.

EUCHARIST

OFFERTORY HYMN   VOCATION

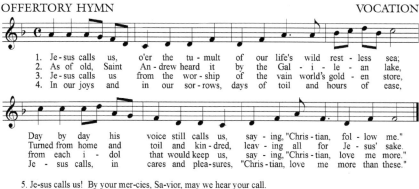

1. Je - sus calls us, o'er the tu - mult of our life's wild rest - less sea;
2. As of old, Saint An - drew heard it by the Gal - i - le - an lake,
3. Je - sus calls us from the wor - ship of the vain world's gold - en store,
4. In our joys and in our sor - rows, days of toil and hours of ease,

Day by day his voice still calls us, say - ing, "Chris - tian, fol - low me."
Turned from home and toil and kin - dred, leav - ing all for Je - sus' sake.
from each i - dol that would keep us, say - ing, "Chris - tian, love me more."
Je - sus calls, in cares and plea - sures, "Chris - tian, love me more than these."

5. Je-sus calls us! By your mer-cies, Sa-vior, may we hear your call.
   Give our hearts to your o-be-dience, serve and love you best of all.

Words: Cecil Frances Alexander, 1852, alt.   Music: F. Russell Mitman, 1996

EXHORTATION — Isaiah 25:6–9

The assembly may stand.

Minister: Lift up your hearts!

All: We lift them to the God of our salvation!

Minister: In Jesus Christ, O God, you are calling us from death into life:
            calling us from the tombs of our despair
                into the freedom of your hope,
            calling us from the darkness of our fears
                into the light of your love,
            calling us from the emptiness of our relationships
                into the fullness of your presence,
            calling us from the everydayness of our world
                into the splendor of your realm.

**All: Thanks be to God who gives us the victory
            through our Lord Jesus Christ.**

Minister: We remember that on the night before his death, Jesus took bread
            and blessed, and broke it, and gave it to the disciples and said,
            "Take, eat, this is my body."
            And he took a cup, and when he had given thanks,
            he gave it to them, saying,
            "Drink of it, all of you, for this is my blood of the new covenant
            which is poured out for many for the forgiveness of sins.

I tell you I shall not drink again of this fruit of the vine
until that day when I drink it anew with you in my Father's kingdom."

All: **Amen. Come, Lord Jesus!**

Minister: We remember also that on the day of resurrection,
when Jesus was at table with two of the disciples,
he took the bread, blessed and broke it and gave it to them;
and their eyes were opened, and they recognized him.

All: **Amen. Come, Lord Jesus!**

Minister: In our remembering, unite us sacramentally in Christ's resurrected life,
that we may be nourished through these holy mysteries until,
with the redeemed of all ages who have lived and died in Christ,
we may feast at last in the full communion of all the saints.

All: **Amen. Come, Lord Jesus!**

Minister: In thanksgiving we hold sacred those faithful women and men
who have followed Jesus' calling and touched our lives with their witness
and whom we now name before you: *name(s)*
Surrounded at this table by your faithful ones in heaven and on earth,
we join our voices with them to sing your praise:

All:

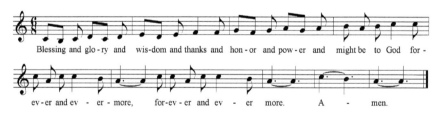

Blessing and glo-ry and wis-dom and thanks and hon-or and pow-er and might be to God for-ev-er and ev-er-more, for-ev-er and ev-er more. A-men.

Words: Revelation 21:12, adapt.   Music: F. Russell Mitman, 2000

Please be seated.

Minister: Together with these gifts of bread and wine, O God,
we offer ourselves in joyful obedience
to summon all who still are wrapped in the death-bands of defeat
into the resurrection-life of Christ's liberating promise:
"I will come again and will take you to myself,
so that where I am, there you may be also."

All: Bless us and bless these gifts that we may be one with Christ
and one with each other in this sacred meal.

All: **Amen!**
          Thanks be to God who gives us the victory
          through our Lord Jesus Christ!

INTERCESSIONS AND THE PRAYER OF OUR SAVIOR
("sins"/"sin against")

THE COMMUNION

THANKSGIVING: *The assembly may stand.*

Minister: Behold, the dwelling of God is with mortals
          God will dwell with them as their God;
          they will be God's peoples, and God will be with them;
          God will wipe every tear from their eyes.
          Death will be no more;
          mourning and crying and pain will be no more,
          for the former things have passed away.   (Rev. 21:3b–4)

All:

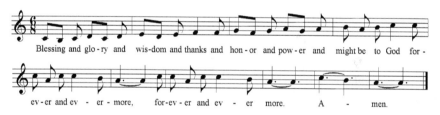

Blessing and glo-ry and   wis-dom and thanks and hon-or and pow-er and   might be to God for-ev-er and ev - er - more,   for-ev-er and ev - er   more.   A - men.

SENDING

Minister: The grace of the Lord Jesus be with all the saints.

All: **Amen.** (Rev. 21:21)

continued on next page

HYMN   REPTON

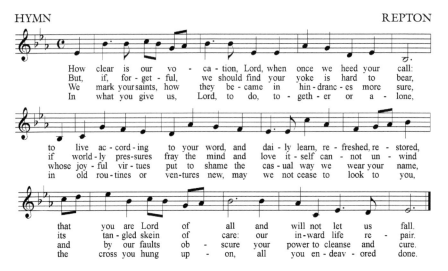

How   clear   is   our   vo - ca - tion, Lord, when   once we   heed your   call:
But,   if,   for - get - ful,   we   should find your   yoke is   hard   to   bear,
We   mark your saints, how   they be - came in   hin - dranc - es more   sure,
In   what you give   us,   Lord, to   do, to - geth - er   or   a -   lone,

to   live ac - cord - ing   to your word, and   dai - ly learn, re - freshed, re - stored,
if   world - ly pres - sures fray the mind and   love it - self can - not un - wind
whose joy - ful vir - tues   put   to shame the   cas - ual way we   wear your name,
in   old   rou - tines or   ven - tures new, may   we   not cease to   look to   you,

that   you are Lord   of   all   and   will not let   us   fall.
its   tan - gled skein of   care: our   in - ward life   re - pair.
and   by   our faults ob -   scure your   power to cleanse and   cure.
the   cross you hung   up -   on,   all   you en - deav - ored done.

Music: C. Hubert H. Parry, 1888; Text: Fred Pratt Green, 1981. Text © 1982 Hope Publishing Company, Carol Stream, IL 60188. All rights reserved. Used by permission. Permission to reproduce this text must be obtained from Hope Publishing Co., 800-323-1049.

BENEDICTION

Leader: Go in peace and serve the Lord.

All: Thanks be to God!

Response: (*singing*) **Alleluia! Alleluia!**

It was clear from the outset that this particular service would be shaped by the lectionary texts for All Saints Day/Sunday. Therefore, among the community gathered, part of the common memory is the familiar hymn "For All the Saints Who from Their Labors Rest" by William Walsham How and set to the tune SINE NOMINE by Ralph Vaughan Williams. Stanzas of this hymn and its concluding double "Alleluias" became a leitmotif that reoccurred several times throughout the service and that tied the individual expressions together. The call to worship was a reading of a portion of the Epistle text for All Saints Day/Sunday. This same text then was transposed as the post-communion thanksgiving toward the conclusion of the service. The third stanza of the opening hymn began: "Ringed by this cloud of witnesses divine. . . . " In order to connect this image with the prayer of confession, I chose to use a complementary scripture text from Hebrews 12:1–2a ("Since we are surrounded by so great a cloud of witnesses . . .) to serve as a bridge between the Gathering and Penitence actions.

The prayer of confession was a transposition of the Gospel text. The phrase "in the poverty of our own profession" deliberately intended to be multivalent. "Our own profession" can mean our acknowledgment of the Lordship of Christ, but it also can mean simultaneously our own practice of ministry. Remember, this was a service for pastors and others engaged in parish ministry. I chose another complementary text, adapted from 1 Timothy 1:14–17, as the words of forgiveness. The choice of scripture texts for what some traditions would designate as "absolution" or "declaration of pardon" is intentional and purposeful. The Word that forgives is a Word that comes from beyond us. Scripture is the best vehicle for this "other" Word, and as the text is verbalized in human words, we pray that the Holy Spirit will speak the *divine* Word of forgiveness to us individually and corporately. The community's affirmation is shaped by a repetition of the twofold "Alleluia" of the opening hymn. An alternative musical response would be the first stanza of the hymn "Immortal, Invisible, God Only Wise," by Walter C. Smith.

In this service the psalm served as the bridge between Penitence and Word actions. To accent the parallelisms in the Hebrew poetry, I decided to have the parallel strophes spoken by two readers, one male and the other female, positioned in the congregation on opposite sides of the chapel. As a response I included some additional repetitions of the twofold "Alleluias" from the opening hymn, "For All the Saints . . . ," again to help to tie the service together. The same response continued following the reading of the Gospel lesson and the scriptural affirmation from Ephesians following the sermon. The title of the sermon, "Doing Ministry Where It Stinks," is an allusion to the King James Version's graphic translation, "He stinketh." As the statement of faith for this service I chose the dialogical setting of the Apostles' Creed, prefaced with the introduction: "With the whole church let us affirm the faith of our baptism." Clearly the reference to baptism reflected the possibility that the Apostles' Creed may have arisen out of a baptismal formula in the early church. On this occasion it also was appropriate to select this particular creed, for the phrase "the communion of saints" would be echoed again in the eucharistic prayer.

On this occasion the images in the prayer of confession and sermon focused the texts on the practice of ministry. The word "call" in the sermon again was intended to convey a double meaning: not only of Jesus' call of Lazarus out of the tomb, but also of his calling the church to new life (consistent with the concern of the text I had identified earlier). Therefore as the offertory I chose to use my own composition, the tune VOCATION, as the setting for the singing of Cecil Frances Alexander's familiar hymn, "Jesus Calls Us O'er the Tumult." My aim here was to allow old words to be overheard in a contemporary musical idiom, again consistent with the concern of the text: "Jesus calls us from death to life." In settings where it is customary for choirs or musicians to provide special music during the offertory this hymn may be used as an offertory response during which the gifts of the people as well as the elements for the eucharist are presented.

The introduction to the meal is a portion of the Old Testament Lesson appointed for All Saints Day/Sunday:

On this mountain the LORD of hosts will make for all peoples a feast of rich food, a feast of well-aged wines, of rich food filled with marrow, of well-aged wines strained clear. And he will destroy on this mountain the shroud that is cast over all peoples, the sheet that is spread over all nations; he will swallow up death forever. Then the Lord GOD will wipe away the tears from all faces, and the disgrace of his people he will take away from all the earth, for the Lord has spoken. It will be said on that day, Lo, this is our God; we have waited for him, so that he might save us. This is the LORD for whom we have waited; let us be glad and rejoice in his salvation. (Isa. 25:6–9)

The phrase "God will wipe away the tears from all faces" echoes the imagery of the Revelation text with which the service began and ended. Both are visions of God's realm, and here the imagery is focused on a feast that God will prepare. By prefacing the eucharist with the words "the Lord of hosts will make for all peoples a feast," it was my intention to open up the text so that *this* meal might have an eschatological dimension: It is the joyous feast of the people gathered at *this* table, but it also is a foreshadowing of the great feast that shall be prepared in the heavenly realm in communion with all the saints. Eucharist, I believe, always is rooted in the celebration of Christ's presence in the community here and now, but eucharist also puts us in communion with Christ's realm beyond our immediate sensory experience. Therefore, the community was invited, in a redaction of the traditional Sursum Corda ("lift up your hearts"), to focus in faith on the transcendent dimension of this meal that would unite them with the whole communion of saints feasting at the heavenly table.

In the eucharistic prayer that followed I transposed again the "call-ing" motif from the Gospels into a prayer recalling God's invitation into Christ's resurrection life. The congregational response, "Thanks be to God who gives us the victory through our Lord Jesus Christ," repeated twice in the prayer was a direct transposition of 1 Corinthians 15:57. The other response, "Amen, Come, Lord Jesus," was a transposition of another com-plementary text from the second-last verse of the Bible (Rev. 21:20). The third response also came from Revelation. Here it was a musical setting of the doxology, "Blessing and glory and wisdom and thanks . . . ," words seemingly piled one on top of each other that lent themselves to an ascend-ing musical motif in the melody line while the accompaniment in the bass line simultaneously descends. I repeated this musical response following the post-communion thanksgiving.

In the *anamnesis* ("remembrance") portion of the prayer I structured the opportunity for the community to name the persons, the saints living and dead, who helped to shape their own calling to ministry. As the names began to become audible throughout the congregation, there was a sense that these saint-mentors became embodied in the liturgical action. The remembrance of them in prayer was cause for an awareness of their pres-ence in the community gathered, a community that is part of God's realm that knows no boundaries of time and space. The concluding words of the eucharistic prayer were shaped by Jesus' promise: "I will come again and will take you to myself, so that where I am, there you may be also" (John 14:3), reinforcing the eschatological dimension of the feast with which the eucharistic action began in the reading of Isaiah's vision.

Finally, the Sending included the last words of the Bible, a comple-mentary text that seemed fitting to close this celebration of All Saints Day/Sunday: "The grace of the Lord Jesus be with all the saints" (Rev. 21:21). This text-transposition was followed with the singing of "How Clear Is Our Vocation, Lord" by the twentieth-century hymn composer Fred Pratt Green, as set to the wonderfully lush nineteenth-century tune, REPTON, by the British composer C. Hubert H. Parry. REPTON, kept alive through its affiliation with "Dear Lord, and Father of Mankind" in British hymnody, thankfully has been revived and set to new words in recently published hymnals in the United States. The concluding response to the blessing repeated the twofold "Alleluias" from the hymn with which the service began.

This was the score that served for the doing of the liturgy in this service for All Saints Day/Sunday. We shall take a look in the next chapter at how scores, translated into bulletins, become the prayer books that enable proclamation through sermon and liturgy to happen.

Rehearsing

Orchestration involves making decisions *before* the final bulletin-draft regarding who will do what and how it will be done. Liturgy is not a monologue. (More to come on this in the next chapter.) If worship leadership is part of the liturgy itself, then the very diversity of expressions will demand a diversity of leadership. It is assumed that the pastor and priest will have primary leadership responsibility in Sunday's worship event, yet he or she also has primary responsibility in orchestrating the parts the other players will play long *before* Sunday arrives. It is rude to ask a person to be a lector five minutes before the service, and it is an offense to God not to give back to God our very best. The last half of the sentence may stir some debate. People like to be asked and like to be asked unpressured by the digital countdown of the clock. (I used to say, "by the ticking of the clock," but electronic clocks don't tick!) People want to be asked to give back to God their very best. They can do so only if as orchestrators we devote time to rehearsing liturgy with those who will lead liturgy.

Musicians have been accustomed to rehearse anthems, vocal solos, and instrumental pieces. They have been less inclined, unfortunately, to rehearse hymns and liturgical responses. Preachers have been known to rehearse sermons out loud in parsonage basements or even in the pulpit before daybreak. Should not, therefore, lectors and liturgists rehearse their parts in the liturgy? And what about greeters and ushers and communion assistants and anyone else in a leadership role in liturgy? I am aware that some in each community complain that laity should not assume leadership roles in liturgy. I even know of a few pastors and priests who guard pulpits and chancels as their private domains. My guess is that such reservations arise because liturgists and lectors sometimes are chosen without regard to the apportionment of the spiritual gifts (not everyone is given the gift of public speech) and are not well rehearsed. Orchestration demands that the ones in whom primary leadership resides devote time to practice what will be praxis come Sunday.

In one of the congregations I served, a husband-wife team was scheduled to usher at Sunday worship. This was the first time they both would be engaged in this ministry. The couple, who had significant resources, engaged their pilot to fly them back home from a business trip in their private plane on Saturday evening so that they, in their own words, "could practice being ushers and do it right." Someone would ask, Why such extravagance simply to practice ushering? The same kind of question was asked long ago when an alabaster flask of precious ointment was lavished on a certain pair of feet. Ushering "right" was one of this couple's many generous gifts that came forth from the depth of their faith. They wanted to give God their very best.

Improvisation

Sometimes leading worship involves not only transposition and orchestration but also, like in playing jazz, a lot of *improvisation,* especially when the bridegroom faints before the altar, and the elder spills the tray of communion glasses, and the organist forgets what comes next, and the sanctuary ceiling falls down like dominoes right before the sermon, and any of the other Murphy-esque calamities that work to undo what had been in preparation for days. Perhaps such comments belong in the next chapter. However, unfortunately, too often what is deemed as improvisation becomes a substitute for orchestration. The hackneyed excuse, "I'm just going to let it all up to the Spirit," is not improvisation but abdication.

Improvisation in music is a learned art. Jazz musicians, playing in ensemble, follow a form in which, generally, each musician is given the opportunity to improvise on a commonly chosen musical theme. Classical organists are taught the art of improvisation, that is, the ability to take a certain musical motif — perhaps a hymn tune or piece of liturgical music — and then to improvise on that given form. Yes, there are times for improvisation in liturgy, times for openness to God's intrusion into our well-orchestrated scores. But there is always a givenness to the shape of the liturgical event and never an abdication of preparation and anticipation for God to do God's own thing.

SIX

Doing Liturgy

The liturgical ordering of the worship event is more than a sequence of words printed in a prayer book or in a Sunday church bulletin. Whatever appears on paper — or even on a transparency projected on a screen large enough for every worshiper to see — those words are only referents to something that happens in the Word-event beyond the words themselves, just as the words of a sermon manuscript or notes are there on paper to enable something else to happen in the preaching moment. The locus of the liturgy is not in the prayer books in the pews nor on the pages of bulletins or whatever those photocopied things that are handed out at the front doors of churches on Sundays are called. *Liturgy is at home in the hearts and the minds of the worshiping community as they do their worship work (leitourgia).* Gregory Dix's exhaustive work in the history of the eucharistic liturgy more than a half-century ago rediscovered that "the ancients . . . habitually spoke of '*doing* the eucharist,' '*performing* the mysteries,' '*making* the synaxis.'"[1]

This chapter is about *doing* liturgy. Everything is shaping and transposing and orchestrating until that moment when the community gathers and either verbally or nonverbally, in whatever language or metaphor, the invitation is given: "Let us worship God." From then on, everything is *doing,* and the homiletical and liturgical preliminaries that have been months and weeks and days in the making now *become* liturgy as the community does their worship work and anticipates the Word of God to be enacted in their midst. All that was said in the previous chapters about engaging the Scriptures, shaping the event, transposing the texts, and orchestrating worship now is focused on that moment when the assembly assembles, the call to worship God is proclaimed, and the community begins to *do* liturgy.

Several precautionary prolegomena are in order regarding this *doing*. Doing liturgy is a human enterprise fraught with all the frailties that are part of our humanness. Yet we do liturgy in obedience to the Christ who said, "*Do this* in remembrance of me," and in the promise that in the human doing the One remembered again will be made known again. Christ is always present in his church; our doing does not make Christ any more present than he already is. Doing liturgy is a human action that opens the community to *knowing* God in Christ through God's own self-revelation. It is a posturing of the community to stand before the burning bush in the anticipation and on the promise that the bush-burning God will create a holy ground. It is a setting of the table in the expectation that the stranger who paused for supper on the road to Emmaus will be present again in the breaking of bread. Doing liturgy is a human project, yet it is primarily God's event. And the mode of knowing that happens is not simply a knowing *about* God, but a *knowing* in a relational sense, in a eucharistic sense, in the Easter sense of Mary's proclamation, "I have seen the Lord!" (John 20:18). Doing liturgy is enacting all that has been shaped and transposed and orchestrated, yet when the call is announced, "Let us worship God," liturgy intends to become God's event. As Paul Wilson says, "God chooses to be encountered."[2]

Secondly, in the metaphors I have used in these chapters to speak about liturgy, I purposely have chosen some and avoided others. Nowhere have I spoken of "conductor" or "director," for if liturgy is God's event, then the One who directs this doing is not the minister, pastor, priest, or any other worship leader. God is free to conduct the divine-human interaction as God wills. Liturgy always rests on the fulcrum of the divine-human dialectic. Liturgy is humanly orchestrated yet divinely directed. It is structured by the shape that Scripture gives to the event, yet it is open-ended to welcome the Spirit to blow through with a new wind and to entertain angels to intervene with other melodies. It is human words, yet it is God's Word. To try to eliminate the dialectic either disintegrates proclamation into easy speeches and liturgy into empty rituals or dissolves all of worship into a mute silence. All have been tried for various reasons and with varied successes throughout the history of religion. This essay is premised on the unresolved tension that Christian liturgy is a human enactment that hopes by God's initiative to become a divine event.

Ensemble

In the orchestration of liturgy I employ the metaphor of "players" and "offerings" rather than "performers" and "performances." Players in an orchestra have parts to play; each plays a part of the whole and interprets his or her score in light of the whole musical experience. Sometimes some players' scores have significant musical rests, when they do not play at all. Although they may be experienced solo performers, when they are part of the orchestra, players are seen visually and expected to play musically as part of an ensemble. Their goal is to interpret corporately the intentions of the composer in the musical score. It can be said that they "perform" in the basic and generic sense of the word: that is, they "do" what the composer has scored.

However, in a culture shaped by electronic media, particularly television, the goal of performance has become narrowed to entertainment, and what performers do in the popular mind is entertain. As Neil Postman has pointed out, "Entertainment is the supra-ideology of all discourse on television. No matter what is depicted or from what point of view, the overarching presumption is that it is there for our amusement and pleasure."[3] The entertainment mode and goal, in what Postman calls "the age of show business," has influenced, perhaps even transformed, the way we educate, vote, and worship. It is the performance mode in worship that is a particular concern to some of us lovers of homiletics and liturgics. Although most worship leaders would be horrified by the criticism that their conduct of worship services imitates show-business techniques, sometimes the performance mode that is so all-pervasive in the culture unconsciously has shaped the ways in which some leaders and congregations do liturgy.

Microphones have made the deaf to hear and given voice to whispers. The opportunities for hearing and speaking that come with ever-improving electronic equipment are mind-boggling. Those who sit in the back — the ones generally with poorest hearing — now can have their own individual hearing devices and the ability to adjust the volume to meet their own needs. Those up front — the leaders — have been relieved of shouting. The "stained-glass" voice — generally male — once needed in cavernous buildings is obsolete. Children now can be heard as well as seen, and can be given voice in worship leadership. Microphones allow speaking and hearing to become more intimate, more relational. The hollering that once characterized tent-meeting preachers is unacceptable in electronically controlled environments.

Yet microphones also have effected some not-so-beneficial modifications in the doing of liturgy. One observable change is that speaking is restricted to the placement of microphones. Even with the advent of inexpensive cordless equipment, many worship leaders have gotten stuck to the microphone places, generally chancel lecterns. I find some worship leaders — clergy included — "conducting" (I am using the word negatively!) liturgy, except for preaching, solely from lecterns. Lectern-liturgies have a way of becoming lectures, and worship ends up being monological, and what becomes monological (literally "one-worded") generally also ends up being monotonous (literally "one-toned")! Moreover, from a theological perspective a monologue is contradictory to the basic affirmation of the priesthood of all believers.

A variant on the same theme is the way in which microphones promote a certain entertainment style of worship leadership. With hand-held microphone pressed to his or her lips, some worship leaders — preachers, liturgists, soloists — have taken to pacing back and forth in the chancel, sometimes poking the device in the face of others, generally children, to amplify their responses sometimes in decibels louder than is comfortable for ears to hear. The model is the television talk-show, and repeated performances reinforce the idea that worship is entertainment focused on some star performers and their manipulative interaction, particularly with children, that prompts laughter — and even applause — from the audience.

The word "audience" has crept into some worship vocabularies. Even though the root of "audience" is simply "to hear," it has taken on a more specific meaning, namely, a group of people who watch and listen to other people's performance — either live or electronically reproduced. Yes, there is a certain kind of relationship that a performer feels between the audience and himself or herself. However, the action is monological: One speaks (or sings, or dances, or plays an instrument) and the others hear and watch. The related word "auditorium" (literally "a place to hear") also has crept into some worship parlance, yet it too is premised on a monological construct. Interestingly, after movie houses sprang up in the early twentieth century, especially before the invention of the "talkies" when organists accompanied the films with improvised theme music, some church buildings adopted a theater-style architecture complete with slanting bowled floors, a stage up front, and draped screens to hide the organ pipes. I know. I was a worship leader in such a building for ten years before a major renovation erased most of its former auditorium-like features — except for the slanting bowled floor.

In contrast to the entertainment mode in which the performer's goal is to amuse the audience, in worship the community, assembly, church, congregation, or whatever name is given to this gathering are the ones who *do* liturgy. Although the community empowers and authorizes certain members to lead the work, liturgy primarily is the *community's* work. And as we stated earlier, the *doing* continually works to define and shape the community. Doing the worship work, therefore, both presumes and defines the community. Unlike a crowd of consumers who happen to find themselves in a shopping mall or a club that meets periodically to pursue its self-interests or an audience that gathers for a one-time performance, the church is church *all the time* — both when gathered in meeting or continuing its work in the world.

Interestingly, the Society of Friends calls each local assembly a "Meeting," and the congregants declare that they are "members of _____ Meeting. The Meeting obviously exists apart from the specified meeting time and has a history most often that precedes and will succeed the particular membership at any moment. And what the assembly-church does in doing liturgy is to enact the words and actions that in the shape of Scripture aim to become the vessels of proclamation through which God may perform the Word. It is in the setting of the community's saying and doing of the transpositions and expressions that were crafted and orchestrated beforehand by their duly appointed interpreters that the texts, in Thomas Long's construct, now say and do what they said and did in their former setting in the Scriptures.[4] The texts are recontextualized in the community's saying and doing of sermon *and* liturgy. The assembly, therefore, as a whole becomes a community of interpreters, the hermeneutical circle is fully closed, and the assembly itself is shaped through the homiletical and liturgical interpretation of the Scriptures into a community of the Word of God.

Further, a community of the Word of God will be an *alternative* community, a community, in the words of Walter Brueggemann, that is "formed and ordered from the inside of its experience and confession and not by borrowing from sources external to its own life."[5] Doing liturgy is participation in an alternative realm in which the crucified and risen Christ, not Caesar, reigns. To a culture and society weary of Caesar's devices and desires, the alternative community is a rather attractive option. Doing liturgy is invitational evangelism. Most people's first point of contact with a congregation is through that church's worship services. Doing liturgy welcomes those searching for an alternative to the cultural idols to which they have sold their souls to step into a new life that God offers through Word and Sacrament.

Doing liturgy is not, however, a dabbling in the occult or otherworldly and does not intend to remove the do-ers from the world. Rather, Christ was incarnate *in* the world and was crucified *by* the world. And Christ becomes enfleshed again amid the human pains and joys that the community brings to its encounter with the Word in worship. Yet *"that* Word," whom Luther points to and identifies — "Christ Jesus, it is he" — abides "above all earthly powers" and renders their idols disarmed and defenseless. Christ and the body of God are not *of* the world, yet Christ and his body are solidly enmeshed in the very created fabric *of* this world. Liturgy is in the world and for the world.

Doing liturgy is doing justice and peace, doing inclusivity and diversity, not because they are the agendas of some currently fashionable correctnesses but because they are Christ's doings being enacted as the community in faithfulness and obedience welcomes their reenactment in the homiletical and liturgical engagement with the Scriptures. It would be an unfaithful contradiction to separate liturgy from its fruits in Christian ethics, and a wanton uprooting to sever ethics from its life-source in liturgy. Doing justice with mercy and walking humbly with God are both in the same mandate. Further, as I indicated earlier, there is a "to be continued" end note to liturgy indicating that the worship service may be over but the service (*leitourgia*) continues as the same texts that shaped the liturgy continue to recontextualize themselves in the settings in which the community lives and moves and has it being. Doing liturgy does not end with the benediction. In fact, just the opposite: The benediction (literally, "good speaking") commissions the community to continue doing God's work in their other life contexts.

Presiding in Worship

In doing liturgy, as in orchestrating liturgy, the community mandates to some of its members responsibility to preside (from the Latin *praesidere*, meaning literally "to sit up front"). The normative "sitting up front" function is derivative from the liturgy and has no being of its own apart from the community. Yes, there are times and seasons for prophets from outside the community, as in the biblical testimony, to confront the community with God's Word. However, from Sunday to Sunday the prophets and priests are community-based, offering the community (including visitors) the opportunity, through Word and Sacrament, to experience God's alternate reality.

Again, as in the conversations regarding the orchestration of liturgy, here I do not wish to become involved in issues of church order and polity. Each community has ways of handing over and entrusting to some of its own the leadership of liturgy. Some will be ordained to a ministry of Word and Sacrament. Some will be there by tradition, and "tradition" in most congregations is determined by the question, "How did we do it last year?" Some will lead by invitation, others, unfortunately, by self-appointment. Yet when it comes to doing liturgy, as in orchestrating, the leaders lead in ensemble with the whole community. In the priesthood of all believers there is no room for prima donnas (of either sex) or eminent domains (either clerical or lay). Ordination to a ministry of Word and Sacrament is not a license to practice liturgical exclusivism. To "sit up front" in the doing of liturgy is a baptismal right (with a "ght" and not a "te") that is bestowed sacramentally on the universal priesthood of all believers. Ironically churches fill up from the back. Adults vie for the back seats while children are the ones who want to sit up front. Perhaps such choices may give some hints on the leadership roles children have in doing liturgy! The Jewish Seder ritual prescribes a liturgical role — asking the four "why" questions — to the *youngest* child in attendance.

Presiding in the Christian community is a baptismal right. Deciding who will do what has to do with giftedness, not as an extraordinary talent, but as a giftedness that can be nurtured by the community for the doing of liturgy. My estimate is that most leaders are leaders through the community's encouragement and disciplining (in the rightful sense of "discipline" as "making a disciple" rather than "punishing"). And many who have been ordained to a ministry of Word and Sacrament were nurtured into a call by a community's need — sometimes in an emergency situation — for someone to help do liturgy: "Barbara, you have been a lector many times. I just got a call from the pastor. He's been sick all night and can't make it to church today. Would you be willing to lead worship?"

I once attended a Good Friday Tenebrae service in which the texts were read by a series of lay women and lay men, while the final passage was read by the resident cleric. Such services depend so much on the skillful readings of the texts themselves to become the sole vessels of recontextualization. I remember this particular service so vividly because the lay persons interpreted the intrinsic rhetoric in the texts far more faithfully, in my estimation, than the clergyperson. Obviously these lectors had a giftedness for oral reading that may have been developed in other settings outside the church, yet it is evident that the decision to choose these particular ones to bear the Word in that particular service was made because they had been encouraged and nourished in the practice of their gifts in some way by this community in the past.

The community generates and empowers its worship leaders. Generally it is assumed that the role of ushers is to assist people to seats and/or to receive the people's offerings. In the latter function they physically present the offerings in whatever manner is customary to that particular community. Rarely, however, do they assume speaking roles. Yet if they truly represent the community in the offertory act, could they not also speak to God for the community? I transposed 1 Corinthians 12:4–7, 12 (from the lection for Epiphany 2 in Year C) into the following offertory act, which specifically gives voice to those presenting the offering.

First person: For the varieties of gifts bestowed on us by the Spirit,

Second person: For the varieties of service to which we are empowered by the Lord,

Third person: For the varieties of ways of reaching out
                  that God activates in everyone,

Fourth person: For all the unique and precious gifts
                  the Holy Spirit apportions to each one of us for the common good,

All: **We offer you thanks, O God,**
            and as members united with one another in baptism,
            we pledge ourselves to work together
            in building up the church of Jesus Christ
            and in showing Christ's love to all the world.

This liturgical act, like all others, needs to be rehearsed by the participants prior to the beginning of worship. A few minutes spent with them explaining what they are doing liturgically as representatives of the congregation and rehearsing the words they will speak is all that is necessary. Every time I orchestrated this particular expression as an offertory response, the people who were involved in the doing indicated that they appreciated the opportunity to have been given liturgical voice. How may we equip and empower others for what are perceived as unconventional roles in worship leadership? Cannot, for example, some be trained as intercessors and be invited in the community's doing liturgy to offer prayers and to anoint for healing? I continue to be amazed by the varieties of leadership roles assigned to lay persons in the liturgical practices in Protestant congregations in Latin America. Frequently the pastor's role is to preach the sermon, and the remainder of the liturgy is led by lay persons.

We come around again to Gordon Lathrop's dictum that "the leadership of the liturgy is part of the liturgy."[6] The doing itself determines who does the leading and how that leadership is realized in the liturgy. The offertory act included earlier is an example of a liturgical transposition that suggests through its inherent structure and language who the leaders may be and how they may exercise their liturgical leadership. Such a perspective defines the way leaders themselves *do* the leading and the rhetoric that accompanies and reinforces their doing. The manner of doing is not some artificial device designed to affect a predetermined experience. Rather, the appropriate leadership conduct (with the accent on the first syllable) arises out of the interpretations and transpositions of the scripture texts themselves. Liturgy determines the way leaders do liturgy so that their doing, and consequently the community's doing, will become translucent vessels that allow the Word of God to shine through them and open up the experience to become God's event. Obviously the leader brings his or her own unique personal gifts and distinctive personality characteristics to the leadership role. Yet the manner in which the leader utilizes his or her gifts so as not to draw attention to his or her personality traits can determine whether the community experiences a translucent moment of divine encounter or, in Gordon Lathrop's alliteration, is nothing more than "the preacher's playground of persuasion."[7]

The manner of reading Scripture, for example, can foster a translucence that enables a text to become an encounter with the Word of God. I learned many years ago from the late Nelle Morton, a theologian and teacher twenty years ahead of the times, the importance of the way the Bible is handled in worship. She always reminded her students that when one reads a text from the Bible liturgically in corporate worship, the nonverbal and visual act of simply opening the book defines that this reading will not be of any piece of literature that is one of the leader's favorites but of Holy Scripture, the church's book. And sometimes where the lectionary indicates that the church's book shall be opened may not be to the leader's liking — nor comfortable for the community's listening. Marva Dawn's striking metaphor, especially for those parts of the service in which the Word is read and preached, is that they "will kill us.... Once worship kills us," she says, "we are born anew to worship God rightly."[8]

It has become customary in some gatherings and traditions for the lector to preface the reading with some expository explanation of what the author was intending or of the social, political, and religious environment in which the text was written. Such introductions cast the pall of a lecture on the reading and become, in some sense, a way of manipulating the community to hear what the leader wants them to hear. There may be times, hopefully infrequently, when the lection begins in the midst of a longer scripture reading and the leader may find it helpful to connect, very briefly in one sentence, the lection with what immediately precedes it. I urge leaders to approach the reading of Scripture with a sense of sacred awe and human curiosity — and certainly not with a "good morning" greeting! The following is an example of an introduction to the reading of a Scripture text.

Reader: The first reading for the Fourth Sunday of Lent is recorded in the book of Numbers, the twenty-first chapter, beginning at verse four. Listen for the Word of God.

Such an introduction not only identifies the text and ties into the larger cycle of the church year but also invites the community into a hearing that emerges beyond the words of the text. Theologically a statement like "Listen for the Word of God" is a quiet affirmation that the Word of God is not bound to the words of Scripture themselves and that the Bible is not to be read as a scientific textbook. Listening to the Bible being read liturgically is a human action of interpretation inviting a hearing of God's Word that comes *through* Scripture yet hears God speaking *on this side of the text* and the speaker. A variant introduction is a transposition of a text repeated in Revelation 2:7, 11, 17, 29: "Let anyone who has an ear listen to what the Spirit is saying" ("to the churches" can be added). The translation of the Greek verb *akouein* as "listen" in the NRSV instead of "hear" as in the earlier versions reinforces the perspective that listening involves a certain resolve of the will rather than a passive and somewhat mechanical functioning of one's auditory faculties.

Moreover, television has trained the entertainment generation to be passive hearers — and if the sound is not loud enough, the volume can be increased — rather than to be active listeners who (pardon the slang) learn to listen up! Some traditions include liturgical frameworks for the reading of Scripture with some prescribed versicles and/or sung responses. Orchestrating these frames or parts of them may help to reinforce that the engagements with the Scriptures are corporate ones. Ending the readings with short statements such as the traditional "the Word of the Lord" or "Word of God, word of life" lift up the uniqueness of Scripture and set the lection apart from the other words that are spoken.

Further, reading Scripture aloud and hearing it being read are intended to be an oral-aural event. We shall speak of oralizing in more detail later, but I want to stress in this context that the reading of Scripture in corporate worship is not a time for individual Bible study and scrutinizing the texts as though one were underlining the salient lines in a textbook on theology. Pew Bibles have a purpose other than to follow along while someone else is reading aloud. The same can be said about bulletin inserts with reprints of the lectionary texts. As a musician I continue to be reminded that it is improper stage etiquette to follow along in the score while someone else is singing or playing. But more than what is proper, reading in one's private Bible is one genre of interpretation; listening to the text being read aloud is another. Joining the two invites a hermeneutical disjuncture such as occurs, for example, when the lector stumbles over a word and the readers in the pews "catch" the mistake. The focus is no longer on listening to the text but on the lector's mistake.

The hermeneutical disjuncture also takes place if the lector reads from one translation while listeners follow along in their own favorite translations or, most often, paraphrases. Obviously the wording will be different, and hearing one set of words while reading another set draws attention to the difference rather than to a corporate listening to words from a common source. Reading Scripture aloud in the assembly intends corporate hearing and listening. I have always insisted that lectors read from the church's Bible, preferably from an authorized translation rather than from some favorite paraphrase that sands off some of Scripture's harshness to make it more palatable to certain theological preconceptions. Something happens in that lively space between the oral and the aural, between the mouth and the ear. That's where the hermeneutical circle is completed. That's where the Word begins to work and the Holy Spirit effects the illumination that allows the hearers to experience words as Word.

Illumination

I am certain that there has been some gnashing of teeth over what may be perceived as a lack of reference to the Holy Spirit in these discussions. It has been an easy device in homiletics and liturgics to invoke the Holy Spirit as a *deus ex machina* either to get the preacher out of a tight spot or to apply a kind of spiritual coating to the words and actions of the human agenda. Certainly the Holy Spirit as the Third Person in the Trinity is at the energizing center of the preliminary engagement with the texts, the interpretation of the texts, and the orchestration of the expressions. The Holy Spirit intercedes, sometimes in sighs too deep for words when the one on whom the mantle of responsibility for the crafting of worship is at a loss for words. All of worship is a plea, "Come, Holy Spirit, come!"

I want to speak specifically in the context of doing liturgy about the illuminating presence of the Holy Spirit in the homiletical and liturgical expressions surrounding the proclamation of the Word. The very private words from Psalm 19:14, "Let the words of my mouth and the meditation of my heart be acceptable to you, O Lord, my rock and my redeemer," have been prayed before many a sermon, sometimes as a last-minute plea for divine intervention to fill in the gaps caused by a lack of thoroughness in the preparation of the sermon. To restrict a prayer for illumination to the preacher's words is a form of self-centeredness. The asking for the Holy Spirit's illuminating presence surrounds not only the preaching of the sermon but also the reading of the Scriptures and the assembly's hearing.

Therefore it is quite appropriate for the lector — whether lay or clergy — to pray a prayer of illumination *before* he or she reads the Scripture and the preacher preaches the sermon. The structural assumption, of course, is that the reading of Scripture and the preaching of the sermon are a unified act. If the focus of the prayer is not simply on "my words," but on *all* the words of Scripture and sermon read and spoken by several speakers and heard by the assembly, then it becomes part of the community's corporate doing of liturgy. It therefore is quite appropriate for this prayer also to be prayed in unison by the whole assembly. Moreover, whether prayed corporately or by the lector, the prayer asks that the Holy Spirit illuminate not only the leaders' words but also effect the Word of God in the hearts and lives of the whole community.

In the following example, images in the Epistle lection for the Fourth Sunday after Epiphany in Year A (1 Cor. 1:18–21) as well as the Gospel (the Beatitudes) are transposed into a unison prayer for illumination. The prayer is preceded by the singing of John Bowring's familiar hymn, the last stanza of which includes the words:

> In the cross of Christ I glory, towering o'er the wrecks of time:
> All the light of sacred story gathers 'round its head sublime.

Note how the images of the hymn that precedes the prayer and the paradoxical metaphors in the lections that followed are captured in the words of the prayer:

**To receive the light of the sacred story that gathers at the cross of Christ,
We ask you, O God, for the illumination of your Holy Spirit.
Open us to the divine foolishness that is wiser than human wisdom,
   and to the weakness that is stronger than human strength,
that we may be led into the blessedness of your realm
   and find the source of our life in Christ Jesus. Amen.**

In *doing* this liturgical expression the community not only is petitioning the Holy Spirit for illumination but also is proclaiming the Gospel paradoxes that will emerge again in the reading of the lections and the preaching of the sermon and later will be enacted in the eucharistic paradox of bread that is not bread and wine that is not wine.

The are many hymn texts that are themselves prayers for illumination. In the following dialogue the words adapted from Psalm 78:23–24 and Deuteronomy 8:3 are juxtaposed with the corporate singing of an adaptation of a stanza of a hymn by Mary Ann Lathbury:

Reader: In the wilderness God commanded the skies above,
            and opened the doors of heaven.
            God rained down manna to eat and gave the grain of heaven.

**All: No one lives by bread alone,
            but by every word that proceeds from the mouth of God.**

(adapted from Psalm 78:23–24, Deut. 8:3)

Unison: *singing*   Tune: BREAD OF LIFE

> Break now the bread of life, dear Lord, to me,
>   as once you broke the loaves beside the sea.
> Beyond the sacred page I seek you, Lord;
>   my spirit pants for you, O living Word!

Words: Mary Ann Lathbury, 1877, alt.

Note how Lathbury superimposed eucharistic images in a hymn text about "breaking" open the Word of God. Rightfully this hymn is included in sections of hymnals focusing on Scripture. It is about the action that occurs when the words of Scripture become the living Word of Christ, yet, in such simple but profound words, it also reminds us that the One Word, Jesus Christ, is made known, "broken," in both Word *and* Sacrament.

Likewise, there are ways of doing liturgy that reinforce the unity of the Word as read from Scripture and preached in the sermon. The *Revised Common Lectionary* appoints some rather lengthy Gospel lections, particularly those for Lent 4, Year A (John 9:1–41, Jesus' healing of the man born blind); for Lent 5, Year A (John 11:1–45, the story of Jesus and Lazarus); for Lent 4, Year C (Luke 15:1–3, 11b–32, the parable of the prodigal and his brother); and the passion narratives for Palm/Passion Sunday each year. These lections lend themselves to be treated liturgically and homiletically as a dialogue, that is, one person reads a portion of the scripture text and another transposes that portion into a homily. The same format repeats as many times as the text itself suggests.

The rhetorical energy inherent in the text shapes the form the liturgical and homiletical dialogue will take. The juxtaposition of portions of the text and short homilies in dialogue is far better than two separate — and long — monologues. This discussion carries over from the previous chapter on the orchestration that takes place before the doing, for the preacher needs to script the homiletical portions of the dialogue in advance so that the lector is aware of where the next reading of the text begins and ends. I used this format for a Scripture/sermon dialogue on the text of Jesus' raising of Lazarus in a congregation I was visiting in my duties as Conference Minister. Prior to the Sunday of my visit I faxed the homiletical portions with the scripture passages inserted to the pastor who was to serve as the lector so that he was aware of what I would be saying and, like a musician during the rests, he would not have to follow along in the score once we began to do the dialogue in worship.

Oralizing and Re-oralizing

In most of human history worship has occurred without prayer books or bulletins or overhead projectors, because what happens when people are encountered by the Word of God is essentially an *oral* event. In his theology of preaching Paul Scott Wilson provides a whole chapter on "Preaching as Oral Event."[9] Again, although my comments will not be chapter-long, we can expand Wilson's ideas to the whole of the worship experience. Worship is an oral event, and doing liturgy involves oralizing and re-oralizing.

Walter Ong has pointed out the radical and fundamental changes in the way of thinking that have occurred as most of the world today has moved from orality to literacy.[10] Corporate worship, however, as conversation and Word-event is conceived of and practiced in primarily oral forms. Homiletics and liturgics deal with oral structures of communication. Preaching and doing liturgy, although nonverbal means of communication are involved, are primarily conversations that necessitate orality. Experiments in Internet "worship" are being tried, yet technology cannot duplicate what happens when people talk face to face. I have difficulty imagining God speaking in e-mail, but I am aware that some of those with greater technological expertise than I have will want to refute my assertion!

PowerPoint, once the privileged electronic tool for organizing the agendas of corporate management meetings and the presentation of business plans, has crept into some churches, particularly as a means for preachers to portray graphically the "points" of their sermons. PowerPoint presentations continue to foster the Enlightenment notion that preaching is a rational argument intended to present information in such a way that it will persuade the hearer/watcher to do something after he or she leaves the meeting rather than a moment in which, beyond words and images, God is doing something right now in the midst and at the center of the gathered assembly. The medium — namely, the video screen — unfortunately is the message when electronics are used simply for the projection of words, albeit electronically written words. I maintain that worship will continue to presume oral forms of expression because they are shaped by the very oral nature of the Scripture texts.

Ong delineates what happens when speech is translated into writing and print. The "dynamics of textuality" change the character of communication. He explains:

> The condition of words in a text is quite different from their condition in spoken discourse. . . . The word in its natural, oral habitat is part of a real, existential present. Spoken utterance is addressed by a real, living person to another real, living person or real, living persons, at a specific time in a real setting which includes always much more than mere words. Spoken words are always modifications of a total situation which is more than verbal. They never occur alone, in a context simply of words. Yet words are alone in a text. Moreover, in composing a text, the "writing" something, the one producing the written utterance is also alone. Writing is a solipsistic operation.[11]

For those of us to whom "solipsistic" may not be everyday vocabulary, my dictionary defines the word as an adjectival form of the philosophical theory that the self is the only reality. Unfortunately, without an eight-cylinder word to describe the situation, some of us have endured solipsistic forms of worship leadership that give the impression that no one else matters, or even is present, except the leader and the words that he or she is orally writing to us. "Oral writing," by the way, is not an oxymoron! And "oral writing" is quite different from the preparatory process of "writing orally" I spoke about in chapter 4.

In the Bible's frame of reference, Ong says,

> God is thought of always as "speaking" to human beings, not as writing to them. The orality of the mindset in the Biblical text, even in its epistolary sections, is overwhelming. The Hebrew *dabar,* which means *word,* means also *event* and thus refers directly to the spoken word. The spoken word is always an event, a movement in time, completely lacking in the thing-like repose of the written or printed word.[12]

Moreover, form criticism has shown that many biblical narratives existed in oral forms before they were transformed into literary genres. As Paul Wilson points out, some of the nuances of their oral origins are still preserved in the grammar and syntax of the scripture texts themselves:

> As in actual speech, individual words and sentences run together, without punctuation or even capitalization to mark sentences. Preference was given to recording sounds that could be reproduced and understood when spoken, not to words that could themselves communicate

directly from the page independent of sound. Moreover, punctuation evolved as an encoded form of voice inflection. In English, "?" means the pitch rises at the end of the sentence and "." means the pitch falls.[13]

The late comedian Victor Borge for years perfected an act in which he assigned certain sounds to punctuation marks and then read a text adding the oral punctuations. The effect is humorous, yet Borge's wonderful piece of comic creativity reinforces the reality that something different happens when a text is oralized.

Doing liturgy is a *re*-oralizing[14] of texts. We spoke of *writing* orally as part of the orchestration of liturgy in the previous chapter. Here our discussion is about *re*-oralizing written and printed forms of communication. There also are nonverbal forms that are not framed in spoken words. Singing a hymn is a re-oralizing of a musical score and text. Signing, as the mode of communication among those with hearing loss, is both a translation into another language (American Sign, for example) and a form of re-oralizing without the aural dimension. We spoke earlier about transposing texts and crafting expressions so that they can be spoken orally, especially in unison by an assembly. Here, all that was part of the previous discussion about writing orally and the orchestration of the rhetorical dimensions of oral communication in the crafting of liturgy now are focused on the actual doing of those transpositions and expressions.

The dynamic nature of worship in African American and Latino/Latina churches is due to the reality that in these communities worship is overwhelmingly an oral experience. Primary hymnody in these traditions resides often not in hymnbooks in the pews but in the corporate memory of the community. Thus, at any time in the worship event musicians break out into song, and the congregation joins in singing. Moreover, with no book or bulletin to be held, a person's hands are free to become involved in movement and clapping, and the whole body can be engaged in a corporate liturgical movement that is a form of dance. The Talmud, although it is in textual form, is still read aloud by Orthodox Jews in Israel and accompanied with a forward-and-backward rocking motion of the torso. Ong reminds us, "The oral word . . . never exists in a simply verbal context, as a written word does. Spoken words are always modifications of a total, existential situation, which always engages the body."[15] Doing liturgy is more than reading printed words.

Paul Wilson says that "a sermon depends upon personal expression, tone, gesture, emphasis, and pace to communicate the preacher's intent."[16] We can enlarge the perspective beyond sermon and preacher to include all liturgical acts and say that those same attributes are critical to the leadership of worship in allowing the inherent dynamics in the written texts to be realized in their re-oralization. Reading Scripture in worship, for example, is a re-oralization of a text that, as Wilson stated above, has residual clues of its original setting in an oral environment. Paying attention to those clues in the texts allows the reading to be shaped by the Scripture itself and enables the text and reader to become translucent vessels inviting God's Word to shine through them. The same is true of liturgists in their re-oralizing of liturgical texts in prayers and other worship expressions. Hopefully the transposers and orchestrators have crafted them in oral language and printed them in oral form so that re-oralizing them flows naturally and allows the rhetorical language written into the expressions to be actualized in the doing of liturgy. Reading Scripture, preaching sermons, and leading liturgical expressions are all moments of interpretation in the community's conversation with the Word of God. So the way in which these are done is integral to the hermeneutical process that began when the crafter first engaged the lectionary texts.

Presence and Conduct

In this section I first want to touch on the issue of homiletical and liturgical presence. Presence in worship leadership involves the rhetorical issues we discussed in the previous chapter that need to be orchestrated into the expressions that will make up the sequence of actions we call liturgy. Now these become focused particularly on those who will "sit up front" in the doing of liturgy. Presence has to do with the worship leaders' *bearing* in doing liturgy.

The account of Jesus' first sermon in Nazareth in Luke 4:16–30 radiates with a sense of his liturgical and homiletical presence in that particular moment. After reading the text of Isaiah, Luke says, "he rolled up the scroll, gave it back to the attendant, and sat down. The eyes of all in the synagogue were fixed on him" (Luke 4:20). Obviously Luke's intention in his own preaching of the Gospel here is to focus on the extraordinariness of Jesus' presence at the very beginning of his public ministry. Yet simply the way in which Luke says Jesus was bearing himself in these actions models a liturgical and homiletical presence for our own preaching and doing liturgy.

The personality of the worship leader is a given; we cannot be what we are not, and to try to do so makes us impostors. Yet beyond personality there is a learnable and practiceable kind of presence that does not render the leader transparent but allows people to see through and beyond his or her presence to the presence of a greater reality. Homiletical and liturgical presence intends to invite people to see what *God* is doing in the midst of the community's doing liturgy. It is not an affected "godliness," but a genuineness and honesty that invites: "If I can trust her, then I can trust God, and if she says God is doing _____, then I can trust that God is doing that." Presence in leading worship is a *bearing* that itself is shaped by the Word of God.

When I was a child in grammar school the quarterly report cards had a space marked "conduct" where the teacher inserted a grade ranging from "A" to "F." "Conduct" in that school environment was synonymous with "behavior." Here "conduct," with the accent on the first syllable, has to do with the way in which worship leaders and the community, in the literal translation of the Latin *conducere*, "lead through" the liturgy. In medieval Latin *conducere* meant "to escort," and I believe "to escort" is a wonderful metaphor for what worship leaders and communities do in the conduct of liturgy. They "escort" the liturgy, allowing the liturgy to be and do in the shape of Scripture what Scripture itself intends to do, so that the spotlight is on the assembly's liturgical enactment of the text(s) rather than on those who do the escorting. The way in which those who escort the liturgy do their work significantly affects and effects the way in which the community does its worship work (*leitourgia*).

Pace is critical to conduct. Timing liturgical speech is like playing music. Music that is played all staccato becomes hard to listen to. Homiletical and liturgical speech that is too fast and clipped militates against serious listening and makes unison speaking either forced or downright impossible. Almost universally I find that the pace by which congregations pray the Lord's Prayer is too fast. It appears that the goal is to get it over with as quickly as possible. In order for children to learn this central expression of the faith and for older folks like me to speak the words with intentionality, the pace needs to be slower. Perhaps the pace of liturgical speech has been acculturated by the media, particularly by the voices behind commercials for used cars in which the duration of speaking is measured in dollars.

On the other hand a leader's pace that is too slow appears labored and prompts the congregation to want to urge him or her to move along a bit faster. In a time when sound amplification was not universal, worship leaders were trained to speak loudly and slowly, particularly in acoustically reverberant sanctuaries, so that the words would not become garbled and the person with hearing difficulties sitting in the back pew could hear. Today's more sophisticated electronic amplification equipment makes speech that is too loud and slow appear affected and outmoded. Television has upped the tempo from what pretelevision generations considered the appropriate pace for speaking.

Likewise, television has increased the timing of liturgy itself. In television there are no silences, except at the moment in a commercial for a luxury sport-utility vehicle that is so large that there is an inordinate silence while the mother-driver searches the cavernous vehicle for her son. Someone once suggested that leaders record worship services and time the amounts of unorchestrated silence. It is amazing how much "down time" there is in some worship services, sometimes more time than is given to the purposeful liturgical silence of which we spoke in the previous chapter. To persons conditioned by television, "down time" not only allows worshipers to become distracted but also encourages the perception that "somebody doesn't know what's happening next around here." Hence, instead of focusing on what God is doing the attention gets fixed on what the leaders are not doing.

It may be helpful also to make a video recording of a worship service so that in viewing it worship leaders can see the gestures and movements that are part of the event. It is easy for unintentional gestures and body movements that are counter to the liturgical rhetoric to become habits. One pastor viewing the video of her sermon noted that she was gesticulating with her index finger. What was intended to be a gesture of emphasis really came off as a scolding finger. One very tall pastor saw himself using arms-and-hands-out-wide movements that became distracting. Again the intention was to convey emphasis, but his own body size militated against these gestures' effectiveness and drew attention to him rather than to the message he was conveying. "Gesture" comes from the Latin *gerere,* "to bear" or "to carry." Gestures are part of the liturgical rhetoric in that they help to carry the liturgy and bear the text in the interpretive process that happens in the conversation between text and community. Movement is inherent in the transposition from lectionary to liturgy. To effect translucence and to let the light of God to shine through the gestures and movements, worship leaders need to be very conscious that their gestures and movements are inherent to the liturgical action and thus are shaped by the interaction with the Scriptures. American sign language as part of liturgy demonstrates how gestures and movements become, like any other oralization, a means of interpretation and transposition.

Vestments and other liturgical attire also are part of the liturgical action. The debate that began in the Reformation of the sixteenth century and has continued in some circles ever since shows how powerful a means of communication vestments are. At times the wearing or non-wearing of vestments has been legislated by both church and state or either. They have been construed as theological statements because what one wears in doing liturgy also is part of liturgy itself. In some liturgical communities vestments are modeled after a priestly approach to liturgy. In others a more academic model prevails. In still others "street" clothing is preferred, although what I see worn on the streets in some places, particularly the graffiti emblazoned on some T-shirts, is hardly fitting for the meeting with God!

Many years ago an elder in a western Pennsylvania congregation had a special suit which he wore only when he helped serve Holy Communion. He called it his "communion suit." The image of a communion suit, in the eyes of this elder suitable only for the administration of the sacrament, reveals that what is worn in the doing of liturgy is part of the liturgy itself. Hence, again, the goal in liturgical attire is not to draw attention to the wearer or to what is worn in doing liturgy, but to allow the liturgical attire to focus on what God is doing. In some traditions it is customary for the church to provide the vestments that worship leaders wear. Perhaps in a time when liturgical attire has become very idiosyncratic it may be appropriate for the community itself to determine and to provide what attire is suitable for the leaders to wear in the doing of liturgy. It is suggested by some that the white garment, generally referred to as an "alb," may be the suitable vestment for both lay and clergy presiders. In some traditions albs are given to adult catechumens to wear for their baptisms and to be retained after baptism for liturgical use. The alb as a baptismal garment therefore becomes a liturgical uni-form (of one form) vestment reflecting the common baptism in which all — lay and clergy alike — are commissioned for service, including liturgical work.

Sacred Space

The community brings to the doing of liturgy a preunderstanding that the homiletical and liturgical conversation with the Scripture will occur *in a place* which has been hallowed by the community and in which there are certain expectations as to what will or will not happen. The place in English-speaking mainline environs is "church." Interestingly, as Gordon Lathrop points out, "Drawn from a transliteration of the Greek *kyriakon,* "belonging to the Lord," the word was first used . . . as the name for a Christian building and only later for the people who assembled in the building."[17] "Church" in English, like equivalent terms in other languages, denotes both people and the place. Although the double meaning has created some theological confusion with terribly practical consequences, "church" as both people and place signifies that the place of doing liturgy is part of the liturgy itself. Churches as buildings are designed, consecrated, and maintained as places where the primary purpose is to do liturgy. In the state where I live the exemption from taxation of church property has been based on the premise that it be used for worship, that is, for a liturgical function.

Volumes have been written on the relationship between architecture and liturgy. My aim here is simply to say, as in the introductory chapter, that the perceptions of how congregations do liturgy determines how they design, build, and renovate their worship spaces. These worship spaces create presupposed perimeters inside which the words and actions of worship will be framed. Sometimes the presuppositions of one generation become liturgical barriers to the next generation. The barriers may be ones that limit the participation of those with physical handicaps and restrict the inclusion of children in worship. One Christian educator took a series of slides showing what a person forty inches tall sees! Worship leaders most often do not have the luxury of renovating liturgical spaces to conform to present desires and understandings regarding the doing of liturgy. So leadership involves adapting the doing to fit the space where it will be done until such time that desire and urgency prompt a redoing of the worship space. I have an architect friend who is a specialist in the "adaptive reuse of buildings." Every worship leader also learns how to become a specialist in the adaptive *liturgical* reuse of less-than-worship-friendly buildings.

The pulpit in the church where I first began ministry is a fine American colonial reproduction of a wine-glass pulpit that places the preacher seemingly halfway between heaven and earth. In a neophyte fresh from seminary, ascending those many steps precipitated fear and trembling; in those who sat in the first five rows of pews the elevation of the preacher induced whiplash. Yet despite its austerity, that pulpit defines preaching, and it communicates to the one entering it the community's intention and expectation: "Preacher, this is the place for you to preach. Now preach!"

The pulpit gives the preacher the community's authorization to preach. Interestingly, "pulpit," like church, has a double meaning. It defines the *place* for preaching (from the Latin *pulpitum,* "platform") as well as the *role* of preaching. "Pulpit" is a platform for preaching as well as the ministry of preaching. There is a current fad for preachers to leave the pulpit and to walk back and forth entertainment-style in the chancel and sometimes up and down the aisles. Not only is this practice a distraction that focuses attention on the preacher, as noted in the previous chapter, but also in leaving the pulpit the preacher steps out of the authorization for the preaching ministry that the pulpit signifies. Moreover, in stepping aside from the Bible that hopefully was opened for him or her on the pulpit, the preacher is declaring nonverbally that there is no connection between the reading and the preaching of the Word and that there is no scriptural authority for the words spoken in his or her homiletical perambulations.

Almost a half century ago Howard Hageman structured his Stone Lectures at Princeton Seminary and their subsequent publication around the images of pulpit and table.[18] In the final chapter titled "Toward a Reformed Liturgic" he was one of the first voices to articulate the unity of Word *and* Sacrament. "Pulpit" and "Table" therefore became designations not only for pieces of liturgical furniture but also for what happens at these furnishings when the community does liturgy. Further insights into baptismal theology gained through ecumenical dialogues in subsequent decades would include "font" along with "pulpit" and "table" as the three loci not only of Reformed worship but of all Christian liturgy. Font, pulpit (in some traditions called an "ambo"), and table are not only the practical pieces of equipment necessary for the doing of liturgy, but they are also the liturgical loci that focus the community's action on what God is doing in the worship event. Font, pulpit, and table continue to communicate to anyone entering the designated and consecrated worship space, even when the community is not gathered for worship, that this community expects to meet the triune God through the sign-acts of baptism, proclamation, and eucharist to which these symbols point. And when the community does gather, doing liturgy centers the community around font, pulpit, and table.

Some liturgically innovative and theologically sensitive architects have designed or redesigned worship spaces that focus attention on font, pulpit, and table. Good architecture makes doing liturgy easy, because the architecture itself is part of the liturgy. Worship spaces left over from a differing conception of worship present a challenge for doing liturgy with integrity and sensitivity. One elder in a congregation I served remarked about the architecture of the church, "This church was an architect's dream, a builder's challenge, and the congregation's nightmare." That nightmare was transformed into a wonderful worship space through the work of a gifted architectural team, a congregation willing to learn and to be open to new ideas, and a leadership collegium that was willing to spend many hours on the project.

However, even the most challenging space can be altered minimally to allow a community to do liturgy with integrity. Most often the modifications are not the physical ones but changes in the way leaders and the community do liturgy. I spoke earlier about microphones and the way in which they limit movement, often forcing liturgical leadership to take place solely from the lectern. By the way, lecterns are really superfluous pieces of furniture that came into churches for reasons about which today most people do not care. Pulpits, not lecterns, are the places for reading and preaching the Word. The Bible belongs on the pulpit. Pulpits, depending on the architecture, can also be secondary places for prayer. About the only thing lecterns are good for is announcements, and they are not a part of liturgy.

The table (or altar, or communion table, or altar table, depending on what certain ecclesiastical traditions and local customs call it) is first of all the place for eucharist/Holy Communion. Although by the end of the Middle Ages altars had become affixed to the east wall of the chancel, Calvin put out a table in the front of the chancel or on the floor in front of the chancel so that the communicants could gather around the table and the one presiding could stand behind the table facing the congregation. The same renovation took place four hundred years later in the Roman Catholic Church following the liturgical reforms of the Second Vatican Council in the 1960s, and the behind-the-table posture now is normative for those who preside in liturgy in both Protestant and Roman Catholic churches. Where it is impossible physically or congregations are unwilling to move altars away from the back wall, Calvin's solution still works well: Place a table in front of the chancel for the celebration of the eucharist.

Secondly the table is the place for prayer — for confession, intercession, and thanksgiving. In sixteenth-century Strassburg under Calvin's leadership, Nichols reports, the minister stood at the table for the prayer of confession and words of assurance and following the sermon — proclaimed from the pulpit — returned to the table to lead the intercessions, prepare the elements, and lead the eucharistic prayer.[19] It is interesting to note how much of the service except for the reading and preaching took place at the table in Calvin's understanding of liturgy. And what was the practice then, after a four-hundred-year hiatus while the church was distracted in other things, has been revived in both Catholic and Protestant communities since the liturgical renewal movement following the Second Vatican Council. The table again is the appropriate place not only for eucharist but also for the prayers that comprise a significant portion of the liturgical action.

One of the exercises I do when I visit a church is to look around to see where the baptismal font is placed. In some places I don't find one or, worse yet, I find it in a closet or pushed into some out-of-the way place because, I am told, "this is an old congregation and we don't have many baptisms any more." In such a view the font is only a piece of furniture rather than the central symbol that continually reminds the community of their belonging to Christ and to one another. It is custom in some traditions for a bowl of holy water to be placed at the entrance to the church. Worshipers are encouraged to dip their hands into the water and make the sign of the cross as a reminder of their baptism into the death and resurrection of Jesus Christ.

In many denominationally produced collections of worship resources there are optional services of remembrance of baptism in which the community engages in a liturgical act of remembrance. It is not a rebaptizing since being initiated into the Christian church is a one-time and for-all-time act. Rather, these occasions, especially when the focus of the Scriptures is on baptism such as on the First Sunday after Epiphany (the Baptism of Jesus) and in the Great Vigil of Easter, become opportunities for the community to recall their baptismal belonging. At other times the leader may begin worship at the font, and pour water into it, as a visual — and even auditory — symbol of the community's initiation into the death and resurrection of Christ. The practice of dipping water from the font and sprinkling it with evergreen branches over the assembly (asperges) is becoming more widespread. Worship begins in some churches with the whole assembly gathered around the font. In funeral or memorial services the commendation may be spoken from the font enacting the scriptural proclamation that in Christ "when you were buried with him in baptism, you were also raised with him through faith in the power of God, who raised him from the dead" (Col. 2:12). In liturgy fonts should never run dry and never be covered over with lids that hide the water. If a new font is constructed, I suggest that the bowl be made of glass so that the water can be seen by the assembly and thus serve as a continual visual reminder of their baptism.

A member of one of the churches I served said to me, "Every time I come into this place I feel as though I am in heaven." The sacred spaces that communities carve out of a secular world and consecrate to the worship of God are, like the people who assemble there, outposts of heaven. For, as St. Paul said, "Our citizenship is in heaven" (Phil. 3:20). Churches of the Orthodox tradition are designed and purposed through their iconography and other furnishings to be places of heaven on earth, and the Divine Liturgy enacted in those places is in itself intended to be a proleptic participation on earth in heavenly realities. Sacred spaces, therefore, are rightfully called "sanctuaries," holy places, where people hope and expect holy things to happen. Further, as sanctuaries these holy places are safe places — safe from Caesar's legions, safe from the state's invasions, safe from consumerism's idols — where in the safety of the Gospel the alternative community may do that which, in Marva Dawn's words, immerses them in the splendor of God.

The Bulletins of Common Prayer

The medium for many transpositions of biblical texts into liturgical acts today is something that has received classification as "the bulletin." In many mainline Protestant worship settings bulletins — or whatever other name is given to those ubiquitous printed things — are necessary for the doing of liturgy. I parodied the title of the classic English prayer book in a chapter heading, "The Bulletins of Common Prayer," which I used in the collection of worship resources published some years ago as *Worship Vessels,* which has been revised and enlarged as *Immersed in the Splendor of God: Resources for Worship Renewal.*[20] I give myself permission to borrow the parody again as the theme of this discussion.

For most of human history, and continuing in some communities into the present, liturgy has been done in oral modes. The expressions which may have been manuscripted by hand for the few trained in literate skills were learned by the majority through oral repetition and passed on to another generation through oral memorization. Johann Gutenberg, a goldsmith and businessman in Mainz, Germany, is credited with the invention of moveable type somewhere between 1440 and 1445. Gutenberg's invention made a *book* of *common* prayer possible, and liturgy moved from oral and aural forms into literary and participatory modes. The liturgical renewal that accompanied the Reformation of the sixteenth century happened through the production and dissemination of printed prayer books. And one can say that the Reformation was possible only because of the mass dissemination of information that occurred through the printing of books.

In 1884 a Chicago businessman by the name of A. B. Dick invented a duplicating process that made prayer books obsolete. Dick's "mimeograph" enabled the crafter of the liturgy to create a new prayer book for each Sunday. Weekly printed bulletins, which heretofore were possible only in well-heeled churches, now became standard fare in even the smallest congregations. Many a pastor was subjected to the Saturday-night curse of the "holy roller" and drugged by the ether-like smell of the blue correction fluid that filled the holes of typos "cut" into the stencils by pounding typewriter keys.

Another era in liturgical history has dawned in the past decades with the development of inexpensive word processing and desktop publishing systems. Now, with a simple photocopier or computer-interfaced printer — perhaps also adding a flat-bed digital scanner — the worship leader can publish a first-class prayer book for each Sunday that may include musical and graphic expressions. Worship resources are available on the Internet, and the worship leader only needs to know how to copy and paste expressions electronically into a format for liturgy. Whole liturgies are available either downloaded from the Web or from "prayer books" on CD-ROMs. Today the crafter of the liturgy not only is freed from the book but also from a typist and the smell of the blue fluid! Wonderful opportunities for the crafting of liturgy lie within the touch of an electronic keyboard and the click of that new breed of church mouse.

The bulletin is more than a listing of worship acts or a directory of where they may be found in other books. The bulletin itself can become the medium for the message. It can become a means of participation in the very conversation of liturgy itself. So it is not uncommon for the word "liturgy" to designate both the *action* of doing liturgy and the *printed order* necessary for the corporate doing of liturgy. The bulletin's intention, like any printed liturgical text, is to be translated by the worshiping congregation from something that is in printed form into a liturgical enactment of what is printed. Crafting the liturgy involves the art of putting the words onto the page in such a way that the bulletin facilitates the enactment. In so doing, the bulletin itself becomes part of the liturgical event. McLuhan was right: *The medium is the message.* [21]

Mimeograph-produced bulletins were restricted by the limitations of mechanical technology. Typewriters, sans ribbons, literally "cut holes" in a stencil that would allow ink to flow through the holes and onto the paper in the mimeograph machine. Typewriters lined up words along the left-hand margin. Most bulletins of this era were directories of where to find the liturgical expressions. The type was, until the advent of daisy wheels, all of one style and pitch. There were only two avenues of emphasis available to the typist: either underlining words or typing them all in capital letters. Bulletins of the directory-type looked like this:

<u>ORDER OF WORSHIP</u>

```
   ORGAN PRELUDE
   CALL TO WORSHIP, No. 4, p. 130
 * HYMN NO. 123
 * CALL TO CONFESSION
 * CONFESSION OF SIN, No. 1, p. 171
 * WORDS OF ASSURANCE
 * RESPONSIVE PSALM, No. 2, p. 253
```

Today computerized word processing provides an almost infinite variety of fonts and formats. Most churches have installed and utilize the new equipment, yet I still see bulletins that, although they have been typed on a computer keyboard, still are in the typewriter mode: Everything is aligned along the left-hand margin, headings are underlined, and corporate expressions are typed all in capital letters, often in block paragraphs. Research has proved that reading texts all in caps is far more difficult than reading words printed in a combination of upper- and lower-case letters. Furthermore, with proportional spacing capital letters consume more space than lower case letters.

To encourage re-oralizing in the doing of liturgy words need to be printed in such a way that corporate speech becomes possible. Each line of speech is determined, therefore, not by how many characters can fit on one line of type but by what can be vocalized by a group of people in one phrase. The same liturgical expressions printed in the typewriter mode above now can appear in a bulletin in the following form:

ORDER OF WORSHIP

Leader: This is the day the Lord has made!

All: **Let us rejoice and be glad in it!**

The assembly may stand.

HYMN NO. 123

CONFESSION OF SIN: *in unison*

       Have mercy upon us, O God,
         according to your loving kindness:
       According to the multitude of your tender mercies
         blot out our transgressions.
       Wash us thoroughly from our iniquities,
         and cleanse us from our sins.
       For we acknowledge our transgressions,
         and our sin is ever before us.
       Create in us clean hearts, O God,
         and renew a right spirit within us;
         through Jesus Christ our Lord. Amen.

Leader: Listen to the comforting assurance of the grace of God
            promised in the Gospel to all who repent and believe:
            Whoever is in Christ is a new creation: Everything old has passed away;
            Behold, everything has become new!
            All this is from God, who reconciled us through Christ,
            and has given us the ministry of reconciliation.   (1 Cor. 5:17–18, alt.)

All: **We believe the good news! Thanks be to God!**

PSALM:

Leader: O Lord, our Sovereign, how majestic is your name in all the earth!

All: **You have set your glory above the heavens....**

To facilitate such re-oralizing, the size of the page of the bulletin becomes a major consideration. In the past most bulletins were printed on 8 ½ x 11 inch paper folded in half. This format provides pages 8 ½ inches long by 5 ½ inches wide. The one line of the psalm in the previous illustration is too long to be printed on such a narrow page. Stock bulletin covers and those prepared by denominational agencies now are available in 8 ½ x 14-inch paper. This size, folded in half, provides pages that are 8 ½ inches long by 7 inches wide. That extra inch and a half per half-page provides 20 percent more room and allows for the printing of lines that may not fit on the smaller paper. Some churches now utilize 11 x 17 inch paper folded in half. Thus, each page is the equivalent of an 8 ½ by 11 inch sheet of paper. This format provides even more space for even larger type.

Moreover, if the bulletin is to become truly *the* one common book for worship for each Sunday, then the bulletin will, of necessity, take on more pages than two half-sides of an 8½ x 11 inch piece of paper. Obviously, the inclusion of music and other liturgical materials necessitates that the bulletin become a booklet of multiple pages. Inserts have a way of falling out and getting in the way of the flow of liturgy. I find it best to print as many pages in order as necessary to include all the worship expressions, and then other pages of announcements and news items can be printed on the successive pages. After the booklet is folded, a staple along the spine will ensure that the pages will not fall out or become confused. Such issues seem mundane; nevertheless the goal is to enable the congregation to participate corporately and to help keep the focus on God and not on the worship leaders.

The computer generation calls such measures attempts to become "user-friendly." Directory-style bulletins that refer the worshipers to expressions that are found elsewhere — generally in prayer books and/or hymnals — create a cumbersome liturgical environment and necessitate a plethora of verbal rubrics to do liturgy. The English word "rubric" is derived from the Latin *rubrica* "red," and originally was a designation for the directions, generally in red type, in missals and prayer books for the way to do the liturgical acts. Today, a "rubric" is a direction printed in the liturgical text itself. My concern here is about the *verbal* directions that appear in so many worship services, such as: "Let us now turn to page 464 in the hymnal and use the second prayer of thanksgiving." Perhaps my manual dexterity has waned, but I simply don't have enough hands and fingers to flip between bulletin, prayer book, and hymnal. My focus is on getting to the right page rather than on opening myself to God's presence. By the time I find the place, the prayer or other expressions already have begun, and my attention is distracted from worship. Moreover, doing liturgy in the directory mode makes each expression a separate piece that seems unconnected to the previous and following expressions. The flow of liturgy is interrupted by the mechanics of hunting books and turning pages. Several years ago a new hymnal was produced for the Evangelical Church in Germany. In a small devotional group one rather elderly gentleman was having difficulty turning the thin pages, and the pastor responded — and I am translating the German literally — "Oh, it pages itself so poorly." I have retrieved that comment on many occasions since then whenever I have been forced to finger my way through hymnals and prayer books.

What is most troublesome about verbal rubrics — most of which are totally unnecessary — is that they not only disrupt the flow of the liturgical action but also focus attention on the worship leader. They end up doing exactly the opposite of their intention. If the structure of liturgy follows the shape of Scripture as outlined in chapter 3, the flow from one act to another necessitates but a few short rubrics that can be printed in italics in the bulletin. On the other hand, if the liturgical structure is cobbled together artificially, the worship leader will need to engage in lengthy verbal rubrics and explanations to effect an unnatural movement from one act to another. In the Great Vigil service to which I referred earlier the bulletin for the liturgy was thirteen pages long. A number of rubrics, including the ones for the congregation to shout the Easter acclamation, were included. The service lasted for nearly three hours, yet never once was a verbal rubric uttered. The rubrics printed in italics in the bulletin were sufficient for a diverse assembly of nearly a thousand people to do liturgy together — including all the sitting, standing, and kneeling involved in doing it.

The same can be said about verbal announcements offered both by worship leaders and by the assembly. Announcements sometimes are important to the community, but are not integral to the worship of God and tend to make visitors feel like outsiders. God has an agenda for the community, but that agenda may or may not be congruent with the parish announcements that generally are made when the community gathers. Most of them are unscripted and therefore consume much more time than the speaker realizes. Furthermore, announcements partake of the entertainment mode of the television culture. One astute congregant commented to me following the worship service, "Russ, there were a lot of commercials today!" In every workshop session the issue of announcements is raised as though they are some kind of necessary evil. Since they really are not part of the liturgical action, I suggest that they occur prior to the service. Then the focus on the liturgical action can begin in whatever mode the gathering actions will take — music, drums, dance, choral reading, spoken words, blowing of the conch shell, ringing of church bells, even, as on Jewish high holidays, the sounding of the shofar — to call the assembly into a spiritual posture to wait for God.

The day is coming and almost now is — and I am sure that what I am about to say more than borders on the heretical — that hymnals also will be rendered obsolete. Photocopy machines and their progeny such as flat-bed digital scanners enable not only the words of hymns but the music as well to be inserted directly into the bulletin so that there is no need to finger one's way through a separate hymnal. I am well aware that hymnals serve a multitude of liturgical, educational, and theological needs; I am not promoting the banning of hymnals. Rather, in the art of crafting liturgy hymnals are a resource that is part of the orchestration phase more than the doing phase. Those responsible for transposing the scripture texts and orchestrating liturgy — and this is the only time I will use the next word in this book — ought to have at least a dozen hymnbooks as resources from which to choose hymns.

We are in a flowering of hymnody, perhaps unprecedented since the days of Watts and Wesley, when wonderful new hymns are being written and composed. No one hymnal can contain this rich treasure. Moreover, the cost of producing and purchasing hymnals limits new editions to about once every thirty years. A host of wonderful new hymnody will need to wait almost to the point of obsolescence to find its way into the worship life of most congregations.

Within the past decade also several organizations have come into being that have purchased copyright permissions from the authors and composers and that, for a yearly fee based on number of members or average worship attendance, grant a license to churches to reproduce any of the hymns included in their franchise. It is now possible, as the Roman Catholic dioceses did when singing hymns was first encouraged after the Second Vatican Council, to include the hymns directly in the text of the liturgy and print them in the bulletin. The pastor of one large congregation recently told me that all the hymns for worship in that congregation are now printed in the bulletin even though there are ample hymnals in the pew racks.

The response of that congregation to the change has been very positive, especially from first-time visitors. A hundred years ago A. B. Dick made prayer books obsolete, and now at the beginning of a new millennium Bill Gates has made hymnals obsolete.

Learning the tools of the printer — and today's user-friendly word processing systems don't demand long apprenticeships — is a requirement for transposing and orchestrating liturgy. A secretary whose job description is "to type the bulletin" not only is, in British English, redundant but also can be a hindrance to the interpretation of the text in its final liturgical form in the bulletin.[22] If the worship leader is creating the expressions by means of a word processor only a few more keystrokes are necessary to put them in a bulletin format that is "camera ready" to be copied or printed.

I am certain that again cries are forthcoming that all this is but one more attempt to manipulate a congregation into what the worship leader — generally the pastor — wants them to experience. Let me repeat that the engagement with the Scriptures, the shaping of the event, the transposing of the texts, the orchestration of liturgy, and the doing of liturgy are never solo performances. Each step involves the whole community's active participation, and each step in the hermeneutical/interpretive process engages the life-texts that each community brings to the event. When such a multitude is included in the movement from lectionary to liturgy manipulation is hard for anyone to come by.

Moreover, not everything needs to be printed in the bulletin. Only whatever is necessary for corporate participation needs to be printed. Obviously the text of the sermon will not be printed in the bulletin to insure that the sermon will not be a "read along with the Reverend." Likewise, whatever is spoken or sung by one person or a choir need not be in print for everyone else to peruse. In a responsive dialogue only the leader's beginning words and those immediately preceding the corporate speaking need to be printed, especially in lengthy prayers that are spoken by the worship leader. The remainder can be encompassed by the three simple dots of an ellipsis as in the following liturgy for the remembrance of baptism:

Leader: Let us pray.

            We thank you, God, for the gift of creation
            called forth by your saving Word....
            Bless this water by your Holy Spirit
            that it may be to us a remembrance of our new life in Christ.

All:	Remind us always of your promises given us in our baptism, and renew our commitment to love you with heart and mind and soul and strength, and to love our neighbors as ourselves.

Leader:	Once we were no people!

All:	**Now we are God's people!**

There are many opportunities for spontaneity and ample occasions for extemporaneity. There is plenty of breathing space too for the Holy Spirit to work wonders even with a computer-generated bulletin.

Some may say that video screens will render hand-held bulletins obsolete. The megachurch movement has mandated large video screens as a necessary component to church growth. They provide the opportunity for worshipers to have both hands free for clapping and other body movements. Yet they are limited in the number of words that can be contained in one screen at a time and tend to restrict the lyrics to praise-choruses of a few repetitive lines. Although a large majority of the population is musically illiterate, there is some value to including the musical notations. However, even the melody line is difficult to read on even a large video screen. Moreover, what about those folks who are myopic? Will hand-held bulletins need to be printed to enable the nearsighted and visually impaired to participate in worship? I heard recently about a church that supposedly has two hundred individual lap-top video screens for the use of people in the pews. That seems like another instance of technological overload. I believe that, despite the novelty of video, printed bulletins will be around for a while, even in growing churches. And, instead of using the screens solely to project texts, they can be freed up to become the medium for projected images that engage the assembly's imagination and accompany the doing of their liturgical work.

We are nearly at the end of these conversations that began with some rather heady hermeneutics and ended with some humdrum housekeepings. Yet amid and between the heady and the humdrum hopefully I have been able to offer some insights and suggestions about what happens in that movement between lectionary and liturgy, between what occurs between the time that the worship leaders open the calendar of Scripture readings and the sexton closes the sanctuary door. There will be another Sunday, and already the orchestration of the next event is a work in progress.

Why do we do all the hard work — "liturgy," remember, is rooted in the Greek word for work — the work that consumes creativity and demands more hours in preparation than the calendar and the clock want to allow, work that engages cadres of people most of whom are offering their gifts and time voluntarily, work that drips drops of sweat from the preacher's brow on the well-fingered pages of Scripture and awakens the organist before dawn to practice that fugue just one more time? Why do we do all the hard work of liturgy? One of my friends who is the organist and choirmaster in one of England's cathedrals was asked the same question: Why spend so much energy recruiting a choir and so much time training them to sing at least one evensong service every day? Why spend so much of one's talent and the resources of the church on something attended by so few people? Reason and economics would have canceled it all more than a fortnight ago. "We do it," Andrew responds, "because we do it for God." Worship is God's event. And even when we don't pull it off very well, God is still there telling us there will be another day, another Sunday.

To be continued.

SEVEN

The Seven Last Words

Whenever a community faces a change, the initial response is what some-one — as a parody on the title sometimes given to the Good Friday lections and an oratorio on the seven last words of Christ by Theodore Dubois — has dubbed, "The Seven Last Words of the Church." The piece always begins when someone sings, "We never did it that way before," and then the whole choir repeats in chorus: "We never did it that way before." There is a second stanza, again in seven words, that is the traditionalists' rendering: "But we always did it that way." "The Seven Last Words of the Church" in either version is a rather popular anthem that at one time or another has been a favorite piece in most churches' repertoires.

What I have sketched in the previous six chapters is about change. Mark Twain once said that the only person who likes change is a wet baby. There is a gene somewhere in the human set of chromosomes that triggers the seven-last-words reaction whenever change crosses the road in front of us. This is particularly true in religious communities where people seek solace against the ever-increasing winds of change that blow through the culture. The more people perceive a certain discomfort and even anger over change in the world around them, the more they want to maintain the comfortable familiarity of a predictable past.

I learned in my conversations with Lyle Schaller many years ago that there are three ways the change takes place: by revolution, by reformation, and by addition. Revolution generally is accompanied by open warfare and bloodletting; it also generally results in the pastor's dismissal and a certain number of the congregants voting with their feet and dropping out. Some-times, however, revolutions are necessary to rid conflicted congregations of the cancers that have sickened them for years.

Reformation occurs gradually, sometimes accompanied by some pain as the tectonic plates of tradition collide with the needs of changing communities. But generally the scars heal over time. Most congregations, most often unconsciously, from a long-term perspective are engaged in some re-formation, unfortunately for some leading to their demise rather than to their renewal.

The easiest way to effect change is through addition. Adding a second worship service is easier than radically altering what is perceived to be normative. Adding another group of ushers is easier than replacing the same old faces. Adding a new worship expression is easier than substituting it for a beloved one. In my own work as a worship leader I have developed a three-tiered category for liturgical change that I have shared with others in workshops and seminars.

The bottom and foundational layer consists of those liturgical elements that rarely change. I do not say "never" because, as the Puritan pastor John Robinson told the pilgrims before they departed for the strange new world, "God hath yet more truth and light to break forth from his holy word." However, change at this level is rare. Liturgically what is included in the "rarely" change category is the basic shape of the liturgy that arises from the very shape of the divine-human interaction witnessed to in the Scriptures, which gives foundational stability to the worshiping community from one Sunday to the next. The shape of what the community practices as their normative pattern at this foundational layer is stored in the corporate, most often unconscious, memory of the community and, when practiced faithfully over years, unites this particular community with the wider liturgical practice of the ecumenical church. These are the truly "catholic" elements that are found almost universally throughout the churches and, as cited earlier, show such striking similarity in Frank Senn's chart. This is the shape of worship that makes the study of homiletics and liturgics an ecumenical possibility.

At the middle layer of change are those expressions that change seasonally. I include in the "seasonal" category expressions such as creeds (and/or statements of faith), doxologies (there are more than the one generally sung to OLD HUNDREDTH), and offertory responses. ("Praise God from whom all blessings flow" does not need to be sung every week.) For example, to help a congregation adapt to the reality that there are other offertory responses than what erroneously is thought to be "The" one and only doxology, it may be appropriate to sing a verse of a hymn during

Advent, with the promise, however, that after the four Sundays in Advent, the offertory response will return to "The" doxology. Once congregations get accustomed to the reality that there will be seasonal changes *but that there also will be a return to whatever is perceived to be traditional* they are less inclined to sing the seven-last-words song. These are the alternatives, arising from the Scriptures themselves, that expand the congregation's liturgical repertoire and can be called up to become season-appropriate expressions that embody the seasonal themes of the lectionary.

The third and top level of change includes those expressions that change weekly. These include hymns, Scripture lections, sermons, and prayers. Nobody expects that scripture texts will not change weekly, and the sanctuary would empty rapidly if the sermon did not change weekly. The expectation regarding hymns is that the selection will be among those in the general repertoire of that particular assembly. New hymns, particularly new hymn tunes, are another matter. The number of new hymns that can be introduced during any year, as mentioned earlier, is rather small. Each congregation thinks it knows what are "new" and "old" hymns. Sometimes, I have discovered, what some members consider the "proper" tune with which to sing a certain hymn to others is not deemed "normal." I gave up trying to have one congregation sing "Blest Be the Tie that Binds" because the congregation was equally divided among three possible traditional tunes. Some corporate prayers may change seasonally; the Lord's Prayer never changes except for language updates that are mutually agreed upon by ecumenical commissions and are owned by the universal church. Other prayers, particularly intercessions and extemporaneous prayers, change weekly. There is a percolating effect that as people accept change at the top, weekly, level, they are more prone to allow some of that change to seep down to the seasonal level. However, the changes that are wrought weekly, to have any integrity at all, are effected not for change's sake but insofar as these changing expressions emerge from attempts to craft faithful transpositions of the Scripture texts.

Change, despite our innate human resistance to it, is inevitable. Without change there would be no growth, no vitality. Marva Dawn names the seven-last-words mentality "the idolatry of traditionalism, which causes us to do everything as it's always been done, to such an extent that worship remains boring and stale. New wine must indeed be put into new wineskins; to try to nurture revival and to be genuinely open to the new movement of the Spirit require that we not be stuck to old forms that have no life."[1]

The process that engages the church in the crafting of new wineskins is what I have tried to be about in this book in response to the question my pastor-neighbor asked more than a quarter century ago: "How do I put it all together?" I am deeply aware that there are innumerable patterns for the sewing together of new wineskins to accommodate any number of "isms" that from time to time are declared to be homiletically and liturgically correct. Depending on what life-experience is motivational some people will find a certain discomfort with what is sketched here. Obviously, my own biases have been less than masked in these discussions. My ultimate hope is these attempts toward a liturgical hermeneutic may provide a way for others to become engaged in the extraordinarily wonderful journey from lectionary to liturgy that leads to worship in the shape of Scripture and invites people in a new millennium to be immersed in the full splendor of God's new day arising.

Music for Congregational Use

The following melody lines may be printed for one-time use in worship bulletins for use in corporate worship. The following permission must be included: Music from F. Russell Mitman, *Worship in the Shape of Scripture,* Copyright 2009 by F. Russell Mitman. Published by the Pilgrim Press. Used with permission.

Doxology

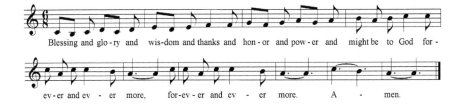

Jesus Calls Us o'er the Tumult

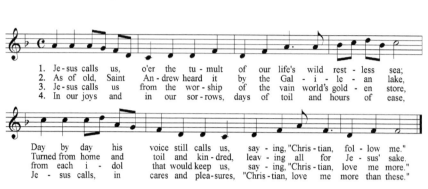

1. Je-sus calls us,   o'er the tu-mult   of   our   life's   wild   rest-less   sea;
2. As of old,   Saint   An-drew heard   it   by   the   Gal-i-le-an   lake,
3. Je-sus calls   us   from   the   wor-ship   of   the   vain   world's gold-en   store,
4. In our joys   and   in   our   sor-rows,   days   of   toil   and   hours   of   ease,

Day   by   day   his   voice still calls us,   say-ing, "Chris-tian, fol-low me."
Turned from home   and   toil and kin-dred,   leav-ing all   for   Je-sus' sake.
from each i-   dol   that would keep us,   say-ing, "Chris-tian, love me more."
Je-   sus calls,   in   cares and plea-sures,   "Chris-tian, love   me   more than these."

5. Je-sus calls us! By your mer-cies, Sa-vior, may we hear your call.
   Give our hearts to your o-be-dience, serve and love you best of all.

Sanctus and Benedictus

Ho - ly, ho - ly, ho - ly Lord,   God   of pow - er and

might.   hea-ven and earth   are   full of your glo - ry.   Ho -

san - na in   the   high - est.   -   Bles - sed the   one   who

comes in   the name of   the   Lord.   Ho - san - na in   the   high - est.

APPENDIX TWO

Accompaniments

Doxology Accompaniment

Jesus Calls Us o'er the Tumult

1. Je-sus calls us, o'er the tu-mult of our life's wild rest-less sea;
2. As of old, Saint An-drew heard it by the Gal-i-le-an lake,
3. Je-sus calls us from the wor-ship of the vain world's gold-en store,
4. In our joys and in our sor-rows, days of toil and hours of ease,

Day by day his voice still calls us, say-ing, "Christ-ian, fol-low me."
Turned from home and toil and kin-dred, leav-ing all for Je-sus' sake.
from each i-dol that would keep us say-ing, "Chris-tian, love me more."
Je-sus calls, in cares and plea-sures, "Christ-ian, love me more than these."

5. Je-sus calls us! By your mer-cies, Sa-vior, may we hear your call.
   Give our hearts to your o-be-dience, serve and love you best of all!

Sanctus and Benedictus Accompaniment

Notes

Chapter 1: Releasing the Word in Worship

1. Don M. Wardlaw, ed., *Preaching Biblically* (Philadelphia: Westminster Press, 1983), 21.

2. James Hastings Nichols, *Romanticism in American Theology* (Chicago: University of Chicago Press, 1961).

3. Fred B. Craddock, *As One without Authority* (Nashville: Abingdon Press, 1971), 3.

4. Wardlaw, *Preaching Biblically,* 12.

5. Gail Ramshaw, *Christian Worship: 100,000 Sundays of Symbols and Rituals* (Minneapolis: Fortress Press, 2009), 6.

6. Gail R. O'Day, "Toward a Biblical Theology of Preaching," in *Listening to the Word: Studies in Honor of Fred B. Craddock,* ed. Gail R. O'Day and Thomas G. Long (Nashville: Abingdon Press, 1993), 18–19.

7. Fred B. Craddock, *Preaching* (Nashville: Abingdon Press, 1985), 147–48.

8. Barbara Brown Taylor, *The Preaching Life* (New York: Cowley Publications, 1993), 82.

9. Ibid., 83.

10. John P. Burgess, *Why Scripture Matters* (Louisville: Westminster John Knox Press, 1998).

11. *Regula* generally is translated and conceived of as "rule," hence the "rule of faith." But *regula* can also mean "measure," as in a tape measure. In such an understanding the Bible is not a set of rules or regulations for faith, but a measure for faith's movement, for how far, how high, how deep, how wide, how long faith may go. The image is that of the old "Regulator" pendulum clocks. The Bible as *regula fidei* sets the arc of the pendulum swing in which faith lives and moves and has its being.

12. Burgess, *Why Scripture Matters,* 53.

13. Stanley Hauerwas, *Unleashing the Scripture: Freeing the Bible from Captivity to America* (Nashville: Abingdon Press, 1993), 27.

14. Burgess, *Why Scripture Matters,* 59.

15. Ibid., 42–43.

16. Ibid., 38–57.

17. Ibid., 41.

18. Walter Brueggemann, *Texts under Negotiation: The Bible and Postmodern Imagination* (Minneapolis: Augsburg Fortress Press, 1993), 26–56.

19. Gail Ramshaw, *A Three-Year Banquet: The Lectionary for the Assembly* (Minneapolis: Augsburg Fortress, 2004).

20. *The New Century Hymnal* (Cleveland: Pilgrim Press, 1995).

21. F. Russell Mitman, *Worship Vessels: Resources for Renewal* (San Francisco: Harper & Row, 1987).

22. F. Russell Mitman, *Immersed in the Splendor of God: Resources for Worship Renewal* (Cleveland: Pilgrim Press, 2005).

23. F. Russell Mitman, *Blessed by the Presence of God: Liturgies for Occasional Services* (Cleveland: Pilgrim Press, 2007).

24. Charles L. Rice, *The Embodied Word: Preaching as Art and Liturgy* (Minneapolis: Fortress Press, 1991), 31.

Chapter 2: Engaging the Scriptures

1. Melinda Quivik, "Re-Assembly: Participation as Faith Construction," in *Centripetal Worship: The Evangelical Heart of Lutheran Worship,* ed. Timothy J. Wengert (Minneapolis: Augsburg Fortress, 2007), 55.

2. William Skudlarek, *The Word in Worship: Preaching in a Liturgical Context* (Nashville: Abingdon, 1981), 71.

3. Gordon Lathrop, "At Least Two Words: The Liturgy as Proclamation," in *The Landscape of Praise: Readings in Liturgical Renewal,* ed. Blair Gilmer Meeks (Valley Forge, Pa.: Trinity Press International), 185.

4. Patricia Wilson-Kastner, *Imagery for Preaching* (Minneapolis: Augsburg Fortress, 1989), 95.

5. Paul Scott Wilson, *Imagination of the Heart* (Nashville: Abingdon Press, 1988), 30.

6. Gordon W. Lathrop, *Holy People: A Liturgical Ecclesiology* (Minneapolis: Fortress Press, 1999), 21.

7. Ibid.

8. Carol Doran and Thomas H. Troeger, *Trouble at the Table* (Nashville: Abingdon Press, 1992), 37.

9. James Hastings Nichols, *Corporate Worship in the Reformed Tradition* (Philadelphia: Westminster Press, 1968), 30.

10. Gerhard Ebeling, *Word and Faith,* trans. James W. Leitch (Philadelphia: Fortress Press, 1963), 311.

11. Ibid.

12. Ibid., 329, 331.

13. David R. Newman, *Worship as Praise and Empowerment* (New York: Pilgrim Press, 1988), 125.

14. Lathrop, *Holy People,* 25.

15. Robert M. Grant with David Tracy, *A Short History of the Interpretation of the Bible* (Philadelphia: Fortress Press, 1984), 181.

16. Leonora Tubbs Tisdale, *Preaching as Local Theology and Folk Art* (Minneapolis: Fortress Press, 1997), 56ff.

17. Grant with Tracy, *A Short History of the Interpretation of the Bible,* 156.

18. Ibid., 159–60.

19. Gordon Lathrop, *Holy Things: A Liturgical Theology* (Minneapolis: Fortress Press, 1993), 18.

20. Ibid., 19.

21. F. W. Dillistone, "Liturgical Form in Word and Act," in *Language and the Worship of the Church*, ed. David Jasper and R. C. D. Jasper (London: Macmillan, 1990), 22.

22. Dom Gregory Dix, *The Shape of the Liturgy* (London: Dacre Press, 1945), xiii.

23. Ibid.

Chapter 3: Shaping the Event

1. Charles L. Rice, *The Embodied Word: Preaching as Art and Liturgy* (Minneapolis: Fortress Press, 1991), 18.

2. Daniel B. Stevick, *The Crafting of Liturgy* (New York: Church Hymnal Corporation, 1990), 5.

3. Ibid., 6.

4. Paul Scott Wilson, *Imagination of the Heart* (Nashville: Abingdon Press, 1988), 23.

5. Dom Gregory Dix, *The Shape of the Liturgy* (London: Dacre Press, 1945), 2.

6. *Evangelical Lutheran Worship* (Minneapolis: Augsburg Fortress, 2006).

7. Kevin W. Irwin, *Responses to 101 Questions on the Mass* (Mahwah, N.J.: Paulist Press, 1999), 95.

8. Frank C. Senn, *Christian Liturgy: Catholic and Evangelical* (Minneapolis: Fortress Press, 1997), 645.

9. Ibid., 46.

10. Gordon W. Lathrop, *Holy Things: A Liturgical Theology* (Minneapolis: Augsburg Fortress, 1993), 33.

11. Senn, *Christian Liturgy,* 646–47.

12. Ibid., 646.

13. Bard Thompson, *Liturgies of the Western Church* (Cleveland: World Publishing Company, 1961).

14. Ibid., 322.

15. Quoted in ibid., 376.

16. Ibid., 381.

17. *I Apology* 67:4, quoted in Gordon Lathrop, *Holy Things: A Liturgical Theology* (Minneapolis: Fortress Press, 1993), 15.

18. Dix, *The Shape of the Liturgy,* 3.

19. *Holy Things,* 15, 19, 33.

20. E. H. Van Olst, *The Bible and Liturgy*, trans. John Vriend (Grand Rapids, Mich.: William B. Eerdmans, 1991), x.

21. William F. Carl III, "Shaping Sermons by the Structure of the Text," in Don M. Wardlaw, ed., *Preaching Biblically* (Philadelphia: Westminster Press, 1983), 124.

22. It is important in determining the structure of this event in the Matthean and Markan versions to allow the story to continue through the next two verses, beyond the traditional stopping point of the narration.

23. Dix, *The Shape of the Liturgy,* 48–102.

24. Gordon W. Lathrop, *Holy People: A Liturgical Ecclesiology* (Minneapolis: Fortress Press, 1999), 47.

25. *Book of Common Worship* (Louisville: Westminster/John Knox Press, 1993), 34–45.

26. Wedding and funeral services that include liturgies for eucharist may be found in F. Russell Mitman, *Blessed by the Presence of God* (Cleveland: Pilgrim Press, 2007).

27. James F. White, *Christian Worship in Transition* (Nashville: Abingdon Press, 1976).

28. Ibid., 10.

29. Marva J. Dawn, *Reaching Out without Dumbing Down* (Grand Rapids, Mich.: William B. Eerdmans, 1995), 76.

30. James Hastings Nichols, *Corporate Worship in the Reformed Tradition* (Philadelphia: Westminster Press, 1968), 23.

31. Marva J. Dawn, *A Royal "Waste" of Time* (Grand Rapids, Mich.: William B. Eerdmans, 1999), 7–8.

Chapter 4: Transposing the Texts

1. Wade Clark Roof, *Spiritual Marketplace: Baby Boomers and the Remaking of American Religion* (Princeton: Princeton University Press, 1999).

2. William C. Placher, *The Domestication of Transcendence* (Louisville: Westminster John Knox Press, 1996), 10.

3. Gordon W. Lathrop, *Holy People: A Liturgical Ecclesiology* (Minneapolis: Fortress Press, 1999), 120.

4. Ibid., 26.

5. Frank C. Senn, *Christian Liturgy: Catholic and Evangelical* (Minneapolis: Fortress Press, 1997), 677.

6. Lathrop, *Holy People,* 64–71.

7. Ibid., 71.

8. Paul Scott Wilson, *Imagination of the Heart* (Nashville: Abingdon Press, 1988), 86.

9. Thomas C. Long, *Preaching and the Literary Forms of the Bible* (Philadelphia: Fortress Press, 1989), 33.

10. Paul Ricoeur, "The Hermeneutical Function of Distanciation," in *Hermeneutics and the Social Sciences,* ed. and trans. John B. Thompson (Cambridge: Cambridge University Press, 1981), 139, quoted in ibid., 35.

11. *The New Century Hymnal* (Cleveland: Pilgrim Press, 1995), 916. One unique and very helpful feature of this hymnal is the index of hymns suggested to accompany the three-year cycle of readings from the *Revised Common Lectionary.* This index illustrates the need and desire of worship leaders and congregations to use hymns as liturgical transpositions of the Scriptures.

12. In expressions that are direct quotes or adaptations of scripture texts, I believe it is important to include the scripture references to show, particularly in an age of biblical illiteracy, that a particular set of words is taken from the Bible. Although I had memorized these particular words from 1 John 1:8–9 through my participation in the liturgy that was part of the weekly worship in the church of my childhood and youth, it was not until much later that I discovered these were biblical words. It also may be helpful to add the scripture references to head off the old complaint, "But we don't have enough Bible in our church!"

13. *Book of Common Worship* (Louisville: Westminster/John Knox Press, 1993), 165–400.

14. Quoted in James F. White, *Introduction to Christian Worship* (Nashville: Abingdon Press, 1980), 213.

15. Ibid.

16. Walter Brueggemann, *Finally Comes the Poet: Daring Speech for Proclamation* (Minneapolis: Fortress Press, 1989), 9.

17. Ibid., 6.

18. Ibid., 9.

19. Wilson, *Imagination of the Heart*.

20. Rodney Kennedy, *The Creative Power of Metaphor: A Rhetorical Homiletics* (Latham, Md.: University Press of America, 1993), 75.

21. Gail Ramshaw, *God beyond Gender* (Minneapolis: Augsburg Press, 1995), 114.

22. Ibid.

23. Gail Ramshaw, *Liturgical Language: Keeping it Metaphoric, Making it Inclusive* (Collegeville, Minn.: Liturgical Press, 1996), 10.

24. Ibid., 12.

25. Paul Scott Wilson, *The Practice of Preaching* (Nashville: Abingdon Press, 1995), 47–48. The chapter "Preaching as an Oral Event" (37–60) includes some examples and exercises to help worship leaders think and write orally.

26. Ibid., 64.

27. Ibid., 78.

28. Henry H. Mitchell, *Celebration and Experience in Preaching* (Nashville: Abingdon Press, 1990), 29.

29. Ibid., 34.

30. Robin R. Meyers, *With Ears to Hear* (Cleveland: Pilgrim Press, 1993), 14.

31. Wilson, *The Practice of Preaching,* 28.

32. Ibid., 29.

33. Meyers, *With Ears to Hear,* 28.

34. Fred B. Craddock, *Overhearing the Gospel* (Nashville: Abingdon Press, 1978), 38.

35. Ibid.

36. Ibid., 13.

37. Some of the issues surrounding "contemporary" worship are addressed in a helpful booklet, *What Is "Contemporary" Worship?* (Minneapolis: Augsburg Fortress, 1999). The chapters include: "What Music Should We Use in Worship?" by Paul Westermeyer, "Shall We Schedule a Menu of Worship Services?" by Paul Bosch, and "How Can Christian Worship Be Contemporary?" by Marianne Sawicki.

38. Marva J. Dawn, *A Royal "Waste" of Time* (Grand Rapids, Mich.: William B. Eerdmans, 1999), 73.

39. Ibid., 67.

40. Craddock, *Overhearing the Gospel,* 38.

41. Wilson, *Imagination of the Heart,* 40–41.

42. *Institutes* 1:4:3, quoted in Bard Thompson, *Liturgies of the Western Church* (Cleveland: World Publishing Company, 1961), 195.

Chapter 5: Orchestrating Worship

1. The chapter by Gordon Lathrop, "Leadership and Liturgical Community," in *Holy Things: A Liturgical Theology* (Minneapolis: Fortress Press, 1993), 180–203, is very helpful.

2. Ibid., 190.

3. Carol Doran and Thomas H. Troeger, *Trouble at the Table* (Nashville: Abingdon Press, 1992), 83.

4. David R. Newman, *Worship as Praise and Empowerment* (New York: Pilgrim Press, 1988), 119–20.

5. Marva J. Dawn, *A Royal "Waste" of Time* (Grand Rapids, Mich.: William B. Eerdmans, 1999), 158.

6. Ibid., 9.

Chapter 6: Doing Liturgy

1. Dom Gregory Dix, *The Shape of the Liturgy* (London: Dacre Press, 1945), 12.

2. Paul Scott Wilson, *The Practice of Preaching* (Nashville: Abingdon Press, 1995), 21.

3. Neil Postman, *Amusing Ourselves to Death: Public Discourse in the Age of Show Business* (New York: Penguin Books, 1986), 87.

4. Thomas C. Long, *Preaching and the Literary Forms of the Bible* (Philadelphia: Fortress Press, 1989), 24. Framed as a homiletical inquiry — which we considered in chapter 2 from a liturgical perspective — Long's original question is: "How may the sermon, in a new setting, say and do what the text says and does in its setting?"

5. Walter Brueggemann, *The Prophetic Imagination* (Philadelphia: Fortress Press, 1978), 15.

6. Gordon Lathrop, *Holy Things: A Liturgical Theology* (Minneapolis: Fortress Press, 1993), 190.

7. Ibid., 183.

8. Marva J. Dawn, *Reaching Out without Dumbing Down* (Grand Rapids, Mich.: William B. Eerdmans, 1995), 206.

9. Wilson, *The Practice of Preaching,* 37–60.

10. Walter J. Ong, *Orality and Literacy* (London: Routledge, 1988).

11. Ibid, 101.

12. Ibid., 75.

13. Wilson, *The Practice of Preaching,* 47.

14. Re-oralizing is different from Ong's "secondary orality," which is primarily the product of electronic media. See Ong, *Orality and Literacy,* 135–38.

15. Ibid., 67.

16. Wilson, *The Practice of Preaching,* 46.

17. Gordon W. Lathrop, *Holy People: A Liturgical Ecclesiology* (Minneapolis: Fortress Press, 1999), 43.

18. Howard G. Hageman, *Pulpit and Table* (Richmond, Va.: John Knox Press, 1962).

19. James Hastings Nichols, *Corporate Worship in the Reformed Tradition* (Philadelphia: Westminster Press, 1968), 44.

20. F. Russell Mitman, *Immersed in the Splendor of God: Resources for Worship Renewal* (Cleveland: Pilgrim Press, 2005), 194ff.

21. Marshall McLuhan and Quentin Fiore, *The Medium Is the Message* (New York: Bantam Books, 1967).

22. For more detailed suggestions in bulletin preparation see F. Russell Mitman, *Worship Vessels: Resources for Renewal* (San Francisco: Harper & Row, 1987), 204–13.

Chapter 7: The Seven Last Words

1. Marva J. Dawn, *Reaching Out without Dumbing Down* (Grand Rapids, Mich.: William B. Eerdmans, 1995), 47.